What people are saying about

Goddess Luminary Leadership Wheel

Dr Lynne Sedgmore is resetting the management literature on leadership, directing it to a new path. Hers is a bold statement: Lynne doesn't do things by half. She positions contemporary leadership as a spiritual enterprise, insisting on incorporating the sacred feminine as an e~~ ~~ial component of successful leadership. Richly ill~~ ~~ 'h practical evidence and timeless ~~   ~~ itten book will inspire you to bet~~   ~~ ld a better place too. **Prof.** ~~   ~~ ding editor, *Journal of Manage~~   ~~gion*, and visiting professor, WU (Vienna ~~   ~~ or Economics and Business), Vienna

This book is a tremendous contribution and stimulus for positive change. It makes a passionate case, and provides meaningful pathways, for a post-patriarchal world. It has a marvellous depth of scholarly insight. It is underpinned by well-founded perspectives that Lynne has gained from the remarkable breadth of her experience, including as a highly successful CEO for many years. We recommend it wholeheartedly.
Lorna Pearcey and **Dr Ian Williams**, co-directors, Caplor Horizons

Goddess Luminary Leadership Wheel provides a powerful set of principles and techniques for spiritually driven leadership. Delving deeply into concepts such as intersectionality, the shadow self and dealing with toxic leadership, this is an ideal work for anyone who is seeking a feminist-based structure of leadership and post-patriarchal concepts of power.
Dr Liz Williams, author of *Miracles of Our Own Making*

In this book, Lynne offers a creative and powerful synthesis of the best of leadership development with an immersive experience of Goddess spirituality. Here you will find a unique, holistic new approach for leaders to birth their fullest potential and the potential of others. I urge you to take this journey. You will emerge all the more equipped and energised to be, and to lead, the change you want to see in the world.

Jody Fry, professor of management and leadership at Texas A&M University-Central, founder of the International Institute for Spiritual Leadership

Goddess Luminary Leadership Wheel is a mould-breaking and interactive work based on decades of priceless expertise. As Dr Sedgmore reminds us, reacquainting women with their true power, in all its forms, and with their intuition, is essential to fostering 'thrive environments'. Implementing the clearing conversations alone would be a life-changing practice for most people. The compilation of the powerful six Luminary Cycles is a lifetime achievement, certain to empower women throughout the world. I can't recommend this work reverently enough.

Trista Hendren, creatrix of Girl God Books

I find Lynne's book quite amazing. I love the Luminary Wheel, and it can be used alongside my own Global Goddess training. Leadership has always been a minefield for women of Goddess. Lynne explores deeply the notion of 'structurelessness' in the collective model, alongside the complex issues of understanding and using power. Working with the powerful principles and techniques offered by the Luminary Leadership Wheel, especially the Shadow archetypes, I am sure many women, especially teachers, will find this book most helpful. Thank you, Lynne, for this revolutionary work.

Anique Radiant Heart, elder priestess of the Global Goddess, Temple of the Global Goddess, Maitland, Australia

Yet again Lynne defines leadership through a new lens. She deftly intertwines and explores spirituality and gender through a focus on divine feminine energy. The bold manifest it and cherish it; it forms the core of their character. This book is a wonderful tool of empowerment for all. Bravo!

Bawa Jain, founder and president of the Centre for Responsible Leadership, USA

This book rocks! The world urgently needs courageous new approaches to leadership and Lynne manifests a vision for our times. Weaving together her extensive personal leadership and spiritual experience, she draws deep from the well of women's thinking and practice, Goddess spirituality and feminist theorising. This book takes us on an adventure into important new pastures.

Professor Simon Western, chief executive of Analytic-Network Coaching and author of *Leadership: A Critical Text*

Previous books by this author
Enlivenment: Poems

Healing Through the Goddess: Poems, Prayers, Chants and Songs
978-1-9997733-0-4

Crone Times: Poems
978-1-9997733-2-8

Goddess Luminary Leadership Wheel

A Post-Patriarchal Paradigm

Goddess Luminary Leadership Wheel

A Post-Patriarchal Paradigm

Lynne Sedgmore

CHANGEMAKERS
BOOKS

Winchester, UK
Washington, USA

JOHN HUNT PUBLISHING

First published by Changemakers Books, 2021
Changemakers Books is an imprint of John Hunt Publishing Ltd., No. 3 East Street,
Alresford, Hampshire SO24 9EE, UK
office@jhpbooks.com
www.johnhuntpublishing.com
www.changemakers-books.com

For distributor details and how to order please visit the 'Ordering' section on our website.

Text copyright: Lynne Sedgmore 2021

ISBN: 978 1 78535 478 6
978 1 78535 479 3 (ebook)
Library of Congress Control Number: 2021916138

A CIP catalogue record for this book is available from the British Library.

Design: Stuart Davies

UK: Printed and bound by CPI Group (UK) Ltd, Croydon, CR0 4YY
Printed in North America by CPI GPS partners

We operate a distinctive and ethical publishing philosophy in all areas of our business, from our global network of authors to production and worldwide distribution.

Contents

In loving memory of my mother, Vera, and father, Mansel, who loved me deeply and always encouraged my fullest potential and shining in the world. In loving encouragement of daughter Keri, stepdaughters Ruth and Beth, and granddaughters Caitlin and Sian.

To all my Luminary students, past, present and future, may you always illuminate and shine.

List of Figures and Illustrations

Figures of key dimensions and models of the Goddess Luminary Leadership Wheel are threaded throughout the book to illustrate different aspects and teachings for further clarity. Each Cycle opens with an illustration of the relevant Luminary Archetype. They appear in the book in black and white and are available on my website, and to students, in full colour.

Figures
Figure 1 **Goddess Luminary Leadership Wheel**
Figure 2 **Luminary Presence**
Figure 3 **Luminary Authenticity**
Figure 4 **Luminary Path of Power**
Figure 5 **Luminary Interconnectedness**
Figure 6 **Luminary Shadow Archetypes**
Figure 7 **Luminary Styles**
Figure 8 **Luminary Shadow Styles**

Illustrations
Illustration 1 **Illuminatrix**
Illustration 2 **Goddess Gnosis**
Illustration 3 **Initiatrix**
Illustration 4 **Ignitrix**
Illustration 5 **Connectrix**
Illustration 6 **Wisdom Keeper**
Illustration 7 **Maturtrix**

Foreword

By Kathy Jones and Ann Limb

Kathy Jones

Lynne was called to take part in the Priestess of Avalon Training in Glastonbury's Goddess Temple. She began to explore ways to combine her extensive knowledge of Leaderful practices with her expanding experience and understanding of Goddess. From this combination, Lynne developed her radical Goddess Luminary Training. I encouraged Lynne to offer her training within Goddess Temple Teachings as I felt it could make a great addition to our life-changing Goddess-centred teachings. Lynne began her two-year Luminary training in 2018, presenting and exploring the revolutionary ideas and practices shared in this book.

Goddess Luminary Leadership Wheel is different, and insightful, for anyone wanting to learn to lead in new and creative ways, centred in Goddess. Lynne's ideas push through the limiting boundaries of patriarchy to create new, dynamic forms of a loving Luminary leadership. We have already felt the effects of her teaching in our own Temple community as trained Luminaries step into new roles. We have incorporated Luminary ideas into our organisational structures.

Lynne presents her ideas with clarity and dedication, creating new paths of leadership for a post-patriarchal world. She has a wonderful ability to describe and synthesise many different points of view that can help transform our understanding of complex ideas. She addresses and questions 'received wisdom'. She brings the new to the fore without making anyone wrong, making everyone part of the change that has to come. This is a great talent.

Her book provides many important ideas on how to transform

1

outmoded patriarchal practices within mainstream structures, which are incapable of supporting the people who work in them. It is time for such an inspired, Goddess-centred vision to take centre-stage in these turbulent times of transformation. A significant contribution to change the world for the better.

In my personal connection to Lynne, I enjoy our questioning conversations on many topics. We are each rooted in second-wave feminism and lifelong spiritual exploration. I have been a teacher of priestesses for the last 24 years, a Creatrix in the alternative Goddess-centred Avalonian world. Lynne has worked extensively in the educational and mainstream leadership worlds. Our different paths provide a rich ground in which we explore ideas, and in which the new flourishes.

My hope is that many will read this book and learn from Lynne's treasure trove of knowledge and wisdom in *Goddess Luminary Leadership Wheel*.

Kathy Jones is founder of Glastonbury Goddess Temple and the Avalonian Priestess Tradition.

* * *

Ann Limb

This is a book about leadership like no other. Its author is one of the most exciting and challenging thinkers on leadership that I know. I worked with Lynne throughout her distinguished career in further education. I witnessed first-hand how much her pioneering and, at times, largely lone voice on the role of spirituality in the workplace became increasingly understood and valued, if not always accepted, by others. Lynne is also one of the most magnificent and loving creatures I have encountered. My personal and professional life has been considerably enriched by her steadfast warmth, generosity and friendship.

Lynne's book offers an innovative definition of what

2

constitutes a leader, or a Luminary, the term she prefers. She proposes a fascinating paradigm of leadership practice, holding out to us the possibility of a world in which humanity can be united through creativity, compassion, collaboration and connection to 'Goddess'.

She provides a compelling personal narrative of her own journey, informed by a fascinating historical perspective of other writers on feminism, spirituality and leadership. Lynne's clearly crafted step-by-step guide through the eight dimensions of the Luminary Wheel are rooted in, and routed through, her personal and professional experiences. They are accessible, engaging and novel. I believe they will be of practical use and help to leaders in all settings.

I believe many – including those in current leadership roles, anyone seeking to become a leader, those who don't even think of themselves as leaders, as well as academics and researchers interested in leadership, feminism and spirituality – will be able to draw insight, wisdom, ideas and new learning from Lynne's writing. Her vocabulary may at times surprise and even confound. Her concepts intentionally test conventional theory, without pretensions to originality. However, I would defy anyone not to discover something new from the vast array of thinkers and writers whose work is referenced.

Lynne's writing, like the woman herself, defies definition while simultaneously embodying a spirit of hope and an energy of possibility. This is a book that presents to us a spectrum of light and a source of enlightenment in our climatically challenged, socially divisive, economically unequal and politically fractured times.

Dr Ann Limb CBE is a philanthropist, mover and Quaker.

Acknowledgements

I thank everyone who has contributed, supported and encouraged me throughout my life.

My leadership ideas and practices have emerged from collaborative relationships, experimentation and practice with thousands of colleagues. My leadership world was that of further education for 36 years. I am grateful to all of you, too many to name. You know who you are.

I also want to thank all those I have journeyed with on my conscious spiritual leadership journey, and the spiritual communities I have belonged to, again too many to name individually.

This book would not have manifested without the support and influence of some wonderful people I must name.

I am indebted to Tim Ward for his belief in my book from first sight, plus his wisdom and professional expertise, as well as his perceptive insight and our spiritual connection.

Words cannot express my love and gratitude to my dearest soul sister, Ann Limb, for writing such a touching foreword; she knows me so well. What a journey we have travelled together for so many years. A huge thank-you to Kathy Jones for her invitation to offer a teaching within Glastonbury Goddess Temple programmes. She was the spark that lit my Luminary flame.

I might never have written this book without the long-time professional and spiritual support, and friendship, of Paul Tosey, Bill Torbert, Simon Western, Louis W. 'Jody' Fry, Yochanan Altman, Peter Hawkins, Judi Neal and June Boyce-Tillman.

Special thanks to the first group of Goddess Luminaries who courageously travelled the pilot year with me from 2018. Together, we created a nourishing, dynamic and stimulating community of Luminary learning, experimentation and power. I love, respect and name you here: Alison, Angie, Anna, Anna-Saqqara, Corah, David, Estelle, Indra, Iona, Julie, Katrin, Lisa, Lizzie, Rob, Marion, Rachel and Tania. Thanks too to Susie, Angie, Marion and Katinka for your support, inspiration and wisdom in the birthing of the Wheel. I am grateful to Luna for setting me off on my renewed exploration of feminism; neither of us knew how significant that would turn out to be.

Families are always affected when a book is written, so thank you Keri, my daughter, for our conversations and your constant wisdom. Conversations with Beth, my youngest stepdaughter, encouraged and supported my renewed passion for feminism. I couldn't have completed the book without my beloved husband, John, who constantly supports and nourishes my heart, spirit and creativity.

Stephanie, Jade and Katrin gave me invaluable advice early on; your responses were important.

The Luminary archetypes are illustrated with beautiful images painted by Kat Shaw, a wonderful artist, who created them specifically for my teachings, with great care and creativity. I am blessed, and grateful, to have an expert and creative designer, Lindsay Baugh, who can translate my thoughts and amateur scribbles into colourful and lucid models. She sorted all the technical details of the manuscript, which totally baffled me.

Thank you to everyone who wrote an endorsement; I greatly appreciate your time and affirmation.

And finally, thank you to the team at Changemakers and John Hunt Publishing for all your guidance and support in making this book come into being.

I am grateful to you all.

An Invitation

I know it is possible for leaders to use their power and influence, their insight and compassion, to lead people back to an understanding of who we are as human beings, to create conditions for our basic human qualities of generosity, contribution, community, and love. And I have studied enough history to know that such leaders always arise when they are most needed. Now it's our turn.

Margaret Wheatley (2017, p. 8)

My vision is to birth a movement of Goddess Luminaries with the motivation, power, skill and capability to make our world a better place. Might this be you? I prefer the word 'Luminary' to 'leader' and define a Luminary as someone who births their own fullest potential and the potential of others and is willing and ready to step into leadership. I use the term Luminary to replace the more masculine word leader and all its associations, and to bring about a radical shift in how it is manifested. Luminary means 'a person who inspires and influences others, someone prominent in their field'. It also means 'a natural light-giving body, especially the sun or moon', someone who illuminates.

The word Luminary resonates far more powerfully for me than the word leader. For me leadership is relational and collective, and I have always tried to lead in a transformational way that is different from conventional or individualistic leadership. The Luminary journey is for anyone interested in pushing the current boundaries and understanding of leadership in the world and inventing a liberating and post-patriarchal way of leading. Society mystifies leadership as something belonging only to a few people who are considered better than, or above, everybody else. I view leadership as something that many people have, to varying degrees. Anyone who chooses to can be a leader, especially if they are fostered, supported and developed. The key question is "What kind of leader do you wish to be?"

I hope to inspire anyone asking this question as well as those excited by different possibilities and new ways of leading. Anyone new to leadership is welcome, as are experienced leaders who are seeking new practices and understandings. Becoming a Luminary may also appeal to women who currently fear leadership or have never had any encouragement to become the kind of leader their heart yearns to be, a yearning for something very, very different from the existing and familiar male norms and role models.

Also welcome are activists, or those in social justice movements, who are experimenting with being leaderless or leaderful and who want to be with other like-minded people. It may have particular appeal to Goddess-loving individuals who are called to experience their leadership through the lens of Goddess spirituality as well as anyone interested in spirituality generally and post-conventional ways of leading. It may also interest academics in the fields of leadership, management, religion and spirituality, Goddess spirituality, feminism and women's studies and organisational development. Whatever your context or previous experience, the most important thing is that you feel drawn to being Luminary, as unfolds in this book. I want the Luminary teachings to be part of a radical movement of genuine change for the better. I acknowledge that I am working currently within a Western context, primarily with white women.

We live in unprecedented, turbulent and uncertain times and new ways of leading are needed now more than ever. The patriarchal, capitalist and neoliberal models of society and the leadership approaches they have generated are failing us. Every year we face new challenges from global issues such as climate change, environmental threats, the current and projected loss of biodiversity, and pandemics. We face serious national, local, community and organisational issues, intertwined with the rise and fall of our own personal challenges and changes in our individual lives. I feel really concerned about the way in which more and more people are feeling isolated, and their mental health adversely affected. The continuing negative impact of the coronavirus (Covid-19) pandemic on personal health and on marginalised communities is huge. Nationalism is rising across the world, yet I also see the rise of new social movements and protest groups and a huge thirst and desire for social justice. Many are expressing a genuine desire to challenge the system of oppression of our patriarchal society and many people are acting to effect deep and equitable change all over the world.

The Luminary Wheel offers a new leadership development approach steeped in the sacred female, in Goddess, and involves much more than simply placing desirable feminine attributes into existing male or masculine leadership models and practices. It has a feminist underpinning and is a conscious, radical, disruptive offering to challenge and change the prevailing patriarchal paradigm of leadership. It affirms existing talents, qualities, capabilities and skills as well as unfolding and learning new ones. It is designed for women, men, all genders and none, aspiring to foster wholeness in everyone. It goes beyond patriarchal and dualist thinking and uses gender-neutral language alongside a core belief that everyone can access their fullest potential through encompassing and drawing upon all facets of themselves. It challenges existing perspectives of conventional leadership and offers a radical alternative. The Luminary Wheel is a hologram, which you can enter at any point and access its wisdom.

The Luminary Wheel was created in the flowing, illuminating energy of the Moon and moves through the four elements of nature and phases of the Moon. It is immersed in the capacity to birth and to foster the fullest potential of all and has eight dimensions. These comprise four radical leadership approaches (the Luminary Leaderful Way, States of Being, Paths of Power and Ways of Knowing), which are synthesised with four shamanic approaches (Goddess Gnosis, Luminary archetypes, Elements and Moon phases).

Becoming Leaderful is encouraged through exploring Synchronous, Service, Flow and Emergence within the awareness of everything and everyone being interconnected and working together in collective and empowering practices. The Paths of Power, Ways of Knowing and States of Being provide ways of being deeply present, grounded and skilful in who we truly are beyond conventional limitations.

At the centre of the Wheel is Goddess Gnosis, a direct visceral experience of the Divine as Goddess, as sacred female. For me Goddess spirituality is embodied and sees sacredness in all of nature rather than seeing nature as something to be dominated, exploited or controlled. There is also significant exploration of shadow through the brilliance of dark moon. A range of practices and ceremonies support sacred relationships and celebrations and the bounty and beauty of all bodies, as well as nature's abundance. I have threaded quotes from students throughout the book to provide a flavour of how they have experienced the teachings and the impact it has had on them.

* * *

I invite you to join me in co-creating this new Luminary Leaderful movement and to journey together through the Goddess Luminary Wheel in a genuine attempt to make the world a better place. I hope you discover a compelling new leadership development model and practice that transcends patriarchy and offers a radical transformative path, inspiring and bringing forth Goddess Luminaries all over the world. Women, men and people of all genders are welcome.

Chapter 1

Return of Goddess

Experiencing the Book
Why Me?
Creating the Goddess Luminary Leadership Wheel
Rising of Goddess
Modern Expressions of Goddess Spirituality

Lynne is midwifing a leadership revolution. She graciously holds the gateway open for all who wish to learn new skills and new ways of being in a Leaderful relationship with life and community. She is clear in her message – leading is always from the heart, a heart that is fully present in embodied love for Goddess and for life. Lynne's teaching style is clear and easy to understand. The course offers the opportunity to dive deeply into new ways of being in the world as a conscious leader, illuminating a clear path with eyes and heart wide open. Answering fully in lived experience the question, "How can we work together to create a fairer, more just world that is sustainable for all, where all voices can be heard, where inclusion and diversity no longer polarise?" This is the revolution we so need right now.

Susie, maieutic Luminary

Experiencing the Book

Choose courage over comfort...And choose the great adventure of being brave and afraid. At the exact same time.
Brené Brown (2018, p. 272)

For me, leadership is relational because it occurs between and for people; it is an art rather than a science. It is developed and honed through lived experience and practice. I want you to feel connected to this book, and to me as author. Your own experience and journey is paramount. All I ask is that you show up in the fullest way you can as we travel the Wheel together.

If at first glance *Goddess Luminary Leadership Wheel* feels complex to you, don't let this put you off. I don't expect you to understand all of it immediately. The journey is developmental and is designed to be absorbed and experienced intellectually, intuitively, emotionally and viscerally. This book is the core text for the Luminary Spiral 1 training, focused on individual development. Spiral 2 focuses on being Leaderful within collectives, group processes and learning liberating practices; to be shared in my next book.

The Wheel speaks to different parts of you, as and when you are ready. Some Cycles and exercises may affect you immediately; some you may feel resistant to, or they have little or no impact; some you may need to return to again and again. For me, the most important thing is that you are affected and changed in some way. You feel more liberated, expanded and better equipped to be a skilful Luminary in the world. Growth and development isn't linear: it's often spiral or circular, and it may have highs and lows, depths and spaciousness. Please find what supports and inspires you to begin the journey, read at your own pace and, most of all, enjoy. Absorb information through all your senses. Do the exercises and ceremonies, sing, move, reflect and journal. The more you practise, reflect and integrate, the more you will absorb, and be better equipped to manifest as a Goddess Luminary in the world.

You may decide to read from beginning to end in the sequence in which it is written. Perhaps you will dip in and out in any order; like a pick-and-mix bag of delicious flavours and treats to feed and nourish you. This book is written to be a companion, a valuable resource to journey with, to engage in dialogue with, to experience, as you would any dear friend. There when you need it, offering advice, guidance, wisdom, information, challenge, experimentation, assurance, reflection and practical exercises.

* * *

I am an extrovert and thrive in the energetic flow of groups and collectives. As a tutor I love having a myriad of resources available to draw on, as and when appropriate, according to the group's needs and desires, to assist their growth and learning. The face-to-face course is a sophisticated mix of concepts, information, experiential practices and ceremony commingling with the unique group dynamics, personalities, wisdom, consciousness, interconnection, synthesis and flow. Writing a book is a much more linear process. I have done my best to capture the dynamism of the in-person course experience.

You will find the names of songs, chants, videos and online publications threaded throughout.

I really recommend you take time to listen, watch and move to them when I suggest you do. They will raise your energy and provide a contrast to reading and reflection.

The Bibliography lists all the books I mention. I have also included an Online Resources section for each chapter and Cycle, with all the links for the relevant section. This includes links to online publications, information, chants, songs and videos. They are numbered so you can find them easily.

* * *

I am now going to sing and dance to Eleanor Brown's song, 'A Call to Stand'; you may wish to join me.[1]

Why Me?

So why would Goddess call me to this? Because I love both Her and leadership dearly. A key aspect of my life is to have always been a spiritual seeker, as well as enjoying a successful career in further education. I have extensive leadership experience of more than 40 years in both mainstream and spiritual organisations. I have been a leader, a leadership developer and a leadership coach, and I completed my doctoral thesis on spiritual leadership. I read avidly and extensively on all shapes and forms of leadership. I confess to being a total leadership geek. For me, we lead for something, for our community, for a passion, to make the world a better place or for social justice. I have never led for position, privilege, recognition or money, while recognising that we all need enough money to live our lives. For many years I have been a bridge between worlds, an edge-walker, a change agent, a seer, a servant leader, a follower and a peer. I have experimented as a pioneer, exploring and pushing new boundaries.

I have always seen leadership differently from how others around me see it. I could never accept the conventional, hierarchical, patriarchal, power over, controlling, heroic, individualistic and competitive approach of mainstream leadership. Inside I always knew there was a different and better way, a way in which I didn't have to sell my soul or compromise my values to be an effective leader. From love, loyalty and spiritual commitment I have worked to be of service in a wide range of communities and organisations. I have been on the receiving end of inappropriate or toxic leaders, and of class and of gender oppression. I have had successes and made lots of mistakes. I have never claimed to be perfect, nor do I want to be. Some of my most powerful learnings have been through messing up, not knowing or by making it up as I go along: experiential learning.

I now briefly list my credentials and experience to write this book. For me leadership is relational and collective, and it is vital to recognise that every achievement in my career involved the contribution of others and lots of teamwork, as well as guidance from a higher power beyond my comprehension. I have a nationally recognised record in leading high-performing, financially successful further education colleges and national organisations, drawing on spirituality as a key dimension and contribution to that success. My organisations consistently outperformed all targets and achieved many national and international awards, including the International Spirit at Work Award in 2007. In 2004 I was appointed CBE for services to education and was listed as one of the top 20 UK educational influencers in the Debrett's 2015 list, and one of the UK 100 Women of Spirit in 2016.

I have been a feminist since I was 17 and I am a qualified and experienced teacher. I have also undertaken significant inner work and self-reflection. I am a student of the Diamond Heart tradition.

There is a significant literature on spirituality in the workplace and the place of a leader's spirituality, and how this impacts on their leadership. This has fascinated me for many years as I worked to integrate my spirituality and my leadership.

* * *

In 1989 I had a deep mystical experience, just after being appointed the dean of a business school.

I felt compelled to begin integrating the professional and spiritual parts of my life, and I have been doing so ever since. Surprisingly to me, I was able to do that and not get fired. It has not been an easy journey; I experienced major obstacles, and many attacks, along the way from people I unsettled or who felt threatened by me. My indomitable love of the Divine, and a higher purpose alongside my own sense of service, kept me on track and cleared the way.

A fuller description of my journey from 1989 to 2013 can be found in my professional doctorate, 'Fostering Innovative Organisational Cultures and High Performance through Explicit Spiritual Leadership' (2013),2 and in *Spiritual Leadership in Action: The CEL Story* (2013), a book written about my work by two well-respected professors, Louis W. Fry and Yochanan Altman. Michael-Joseph completed a doctorate on my leadership in 2002, 'Leaders and Spirituality: A Case Study'.[3] They all conclude that my spirituality did significantly support my success and effectiveness.

Serving and supporting others on their leadership journey is my vocation. I have explored and taught every leadership approach there is, from heroic to distributed, from scientific to soul and spiritual, from conventional to eco, from feminist to critical theory. I have worked with many leadership models and different forms of power. I believe everyone has the potential to be a leader if you choose to be one. Some of you already know that and can express it easily and naturally. Others may need encouragement and conscious development. Some of you may enjoy leadership as a spiritual path of growth, as I do. My expression as a published poet and my experiences as a mother, stepmother and grandmother have all assisted me in developing and expressing my own style. I have been a spiritual seeker since I was a child and have explored many faith paths. I was ordained as an interfaith minister in 2002 and was a Benedictine oblate for many years. I am active in the Glastonbury Goddess community as a priestess, Temple Melissa, tutor and healer. I work also as an executive leadership and soul coach. I express my love of Goddess, my love of leadership and my service to others by birthing the Goddess Luminary Leadership Wheel, and this book.

Creating the Goddess Luminary Leadership Wheel

Is anything ever truly original? The Goddess Luminary Leadership Wheel is my unique synthesis and weaving. It is influenced by Kathy Jones's Brigit-Anna and Avalonian Wheels, using her directions, created in Glastonbury, England, where I now live. My ancestral roots are Cornish and Welsh; my surname is Sedgmore, still a name of the land in Somerset. I have returned home to my own Brythonic roots within a Celtic Goddess spirituality tradition. I have undertaken numerous mainstream leadership development programmes and significant spiritual development, as well as training as a priestess in the Avalonian tradition for five years.

The Goddess Luminary Leadership Wheel reframes everything I know, and feel, from my numerous years of leadership experience and my more recent experiences of being a priestess and explorer of Goddess spirituality. It feels important to articulate why I created the Wheel and why I place Goddess at its centre. Goddess feminism arose in me, as it did for many women, as a deeply visceral spiritual expression, an embodiment of the Divine as female.

Goddess spirituality, for me, is a conscious and disruptive choice to oppose and challenge patriarchy and patriarchal religions. Goddess spirituality, as a modern phenomenon, emerged in the 1970s and 1980s. It stimulated explicit critiques of the different faith traditions, organised around patriarchal male Gods, which treat women badly. All male-created religions have an emphasis on domination, violence and war. Yes, the holy books of those religions include love, peace and forgiveness, but they also, unapologetically, treat women in demeaning and unacceptable ways. They frequently portray women as unholy temptresses with limited or flawed spiritual potential, unfit to hold positions of spiritual authority. The female body is viewed as an impediment to enlightenment, or as an object of temptation and seduction that leads good men astray. Patriarchal religions assert this repeatedly through their suppression and denigration of women. They view women as not sacred, inferior to men and unsuitable for leadership roles in their faith communities.

How have I journeyed to Goddess? I have experienced a deep connection with something beyond me and bigger than me since I was a child: a living, breathing palpable presence. Over many years my knowing of that Divine source changed, from a Sunday school God in the sky, to directly experiencing light filling me with visceral knowing of a loving, benign universe beyond gender. I initially knew source as transcendent (beyond self) and had a love affair with God in a dual relationship with my personal deity. As I moved into knowing source as immanent (from within) I journeyed beyond duality and experienced interconnected oneness with an impersonal metaphysical energy and presence of light, love and beauty.

Alongside this I explored Goddess in myth, as archetype and in pilgrimages to Goddess sacred sites. She first became fully alive for me in 1982 as physically, spiritually, energetically and personally everywhere, flowing within the web and matrix of all life. She inspired my feminist activism, as well as being in nature, in my body and in my relationships, especially with women. I also continued to explore patriarchal religions and to try to reform them from within. My direct knowing of Goddess holds paradox, intimacy and deliciousness within the visceral knowing of a loving, benign universe. In my life I have walked to Goddess, and now walk with Goddess and, when fully in flow, as Goddess. Whatever I do is influenced from Goddess experienced as verb, being Her, rather than as noun, as a separate entity.

* * *

My hope and my deepest wish is that more women, men and

people of all genders are called by Goddess. A valuable spiritual path to learn their worth and their value, to heal wounding, to find their voice, their strength, so they can speak up for themselves and find what they want to manifest in the world.

The word 'Luminary' resonates far more powerfully for me than the word 'leader'. Over several months my vision gestated, then began to birth, from sitting with the moon. I dreamed of initiating a new community of Goddess Luminaries, individuals ready to step forward into visible, revelatory and power-full manifestations of Goddess-inspired leadership within the world. Through a Druid contact I researched the word 'leader' back to its Anglo-Saxon roots. It originally means a 'track seer', the one who goes in front, because they can see and follow the animal tracks. By going in front and stepping forward, literally, they became important in feeding the tribe and ensuring its survival. A literal translation is 'seer of the ley', one who can see the way forward, the leyseer or the way-shower. What I liked in this understanding was that leadership is intertwined with the willingness and the skills of following.

I then travelled beyond the notion of leaders and followers and distributed leadership to viscerally knowing that we can all be leaders simultaneously. I discovered the notion of Leaderful and explored it in depth. I also explored Teal or post-conventional ways of leading. Gradually my insights began to flow and to emerge naturally into the shape of a wheel. I further explored and integrated my understanding to go beyond limiting and patriarchal approaches.

I revisited mainstream, soulful, spiritual, ethical, collective, reflective, distributed and virtuous leadership literature. I rediscovered the second- and third-wave feminist approaches and resistances to leadership and reread avidly the work of Starhawk, my favourite Goddess-inspired leadership writer and earth activist. I filled the bibliography for my new course with new books written by, or about, a wide range of female leaders, past and current. I had a fantastic time of exploration and synthesis, some of which I now share with you.

Rising of Goddess

Then she opens her arms to the Divine Feminine, discovering her in ancient places and traditional places, but mostly inside her own self.
Sue Monk Kidd (2002, p. 226)

I have made a conscious choice to immerse myself even more fully in Goddess and to celebrate and express the Divine in female form, training for the past five years as a priestess. This is a significant part of my own healing journey and is also a political statement, as I believe the rise of Goddess in all Her magnificence is essential in the world at this time. The embodiment of Goddess and the sacred female can bring about wholeness for everyone and heal our planet. Goddess spirituality challenges the current destruction of Gaia. Mother Earth, as Goddess, is the sacred ground beneath our feet, to be honoured and respected. She births, loves and protects; she does not dominate. Death is a natural part of Her cycle of life.

For many, Goddess is integral to feminism and involves empowerment for all. Anyone who finds Goddess can experience that they are fully female in a profound way, beyond conventional and patriarchal limitations of gender or binary concepts of masculine and feminine. Goddess interconnectedness can heal any wounding. I want a society in which the choice to experience the Divine as Goddess is actively encouraged and is genuinely accessible without discriminatory essentialism. Essentialism is a belief that things have a set of characteristics which make them what they are; in this context it refers to certain categories, such as women and racial groups, having an underlying reality or true nature and a set of attributes that are necessary to their identity and function.

Many are hearing Her call, in different ways, places and forms. Goddess, or the sacred female, has been or is now being engaged in many fields, including feminism, religion, academia, fiction, sexuality, leadership and popular songs, supported by some celebrities and in eco-environmental movements. Another exciting feature is the establishment of new Goddess temples and communities all over the world. One of the largest and most significant is the Glastonbury Goddess community in the UK, within which I have trained and from which the Goddess Luminary Wheel has evolved. There is a rich and bountiful tradition of writers about Goddess, too numerous to include all of them. I include books whose writers have influenced me most and encourage you to explore themes that interest you from this ever-expanding Goddess offering.

Through the rise and fall of different civilisations, Goddess has been honoured over the ages in many different shapes and forms, emerging and re-emerging within different cultures.

For centuries, women have been forced to play roles based on limited cultural expectations of how a woman should behave. Religion has been one of the most oppressive spaces for women. For far too long women have had to limit, hide or suppress their experience of their own divinity. This restriction has created significant blocks to reclaiming and expressing Divine feminine understanding and power. This is changing drastically as women actively reclaim the Divine as female rather than male only. I remain open to the imagining of the Divine female expressing herself in the broadest possible ways, including both binary and queer. The Goddess Luminary Wheel is designed to connect anyone to their own divinity as Goddess or sacred female. It is not prescriptive in any way. My use of the word 'Goddess' encompasses all the ways in which the sacred female is experienced. Goddess is constantly liberating and unfolding, as well as being who we already are.

As part of my own Goddess spirituality journey, I have needed to explore my own gender identity as a white, working-class, bisexual, androgynous, cisgender woman and second-wave feminist activist of the 1970s and 1980s. For me, the power of universal sisterhood, uniting as sisters across all boundaries and experiencing all women coming together, as women, to fight patriarchy, was a liberating and exhilarating experience. Yet I have needed to embrace the limitations of essentialism, see through the myth of the homogeneous woman's movement, and journey through binary limitations of gender to better understand the complexities and ravages of oppression in all its intersectionalities, especially for non-binary and transgender people.

I want to celebrate Goddess as a necessary development in the continued fight for women's fullest liberation and potential, and to respect and be an ally for all oppressed groups, including transgender people. For me, queer and non-binary thinking encourages expansiveness in which everyone is included, not a threat or an imposition. It is for each of us to find our own understanding and expression of Goddess spirituality; I want mine to be as inclusive as possible. My personal privilege includes access to excellent education, financial resources and vast experience as a leader and coach in many different organisations and communities. The Goddess Luminary Wheel is a culmination and synthesis of my life and a way of offering service from my privilege.

Modern Expressions of Goddess Spirituality

Goddess and feminist researchers have explored prehistory, history, theology, anthropology, archaeology and many other disciplines. Female deities have been discovered and claims made that prehistoric women's lives were not subordinate, and that women's values were uppermost in a female-defined spirituality of Goddess worship. Feminist scholars understand

21

modern-day women's spirituality as a struggle to achieve full humanity through self-actualisation and that patriarchal religions prevent women from realising their full spiritual potential. Feminist spirituality became a movement to empower women towards their own unique and holistic experience of spiritual self-actualisation. I will now describe key themes and some of the women who have influenced me and opened the way for my teachings to be possible.

Matrilineal and Archaeological Discoveries

In the West, spiritual interest in ancient Goddesses is a relatively new social phenomenon emerging from archaeological investigations. Images of the female form have existed all over the world alongside evidence from ancient temple sites, statues, customs, rituals and symbolism suggesting that Goddess worship can be traced from the Palaeolithic period (30,000–25,000 BCE) through the Neolithic times (12,000–3,500 BCE).

Many writers, including Kathy Jones, Merlin Stone and Marija Gimbutas, link the numerous Palaeolithic female figurines with Goddess-worshipping societies in the Neolithic period, especially in the Near and Middle East. The figurines from the two periods have similarities suggesting they are Mother or Earth Goddesses.

Catal Huyuk in Turkey is a Neolithic archaeological site in which a seated Mother Goddess figurine from *circa* 5800 BCE was found. Goddess figurines have been discovered in what are now known as southern Iraq, Egypt, Syria, the Persian Gulf, Greece and Rome, and in every area of the Near and Middle East. Many researchers believe that in all these places Mother Goddess was revered as the deity, and in some places had Her own temples and priestesses. In these societies, the role of women was positive and highly valued. Women bore children, were chief producers of food, had economic and social power and were held in high esteem; land would have been passed down through the mother line. Later, patriarchal religions adapted, destroyed or absorbed Goddess, deliberately erasing Her.

Marija Gimbutas, a Lithuanian American archaeologist and anthropologist, was a pioneer and respected revolutionary scholar on the earliest horticultural societies of Old European cultures. Two of her books, *The Goddesses and Gods of Old Europe, 7000 to 3500 BC: Myths, Legends and Cult Images* (1974) and *The Language of the Goddess: Unearthing the Hidden Symbols of Western Civilization* (1989), have been invaluable in rewriting the narrative of Goddess and providing a new interpretation that supports the existence of Goddess. She reinterpreted the meaning of the Neolithic symbolic language of the mystery of birth, death and renewal carved on stone or on Venus figurines by illustrating how particular patterns and symbols are linked to different faces of Goddess.

The Early Feminist Spirituality Movement

The feminist spirituality movement emerged in the mid-1970s and became a significant strand within feminism. It explored a wide range of approaches and practices, including Goddess spirituality, the sacred female within traditional faith traditions, pagan paths, pacifism, ecofeminism, witchcraft, mysticism and animism. Those not drawn to feminist spirituality felt it distracted from political work, whereas spiritual feminists viewed their work as both personal and political, especially on anti-nuclear and environmental issues. For many, spirituality was a much-needed source of rejuvenation and nourishment to enable continued political struggle and to prevent burnout. For many in left-wing politics, spirituality was a definite no-go area. Gradually, for some Goddess-loving women the political focus of the 1990s no longer felt relevant and they began to withdraw from the concerns of the mainstream world to live alternative lifestyles. A key part of my Luminary teachings is to reclaim this herstory and the conscious choice of Goddess spirituality as a spiritual path and, for those who wish, to explore an explicit feminist, radical, disruptive political path.

Wicca

The witches, female healers, wise women, crones and midwives, however harmed by patriarchy, have remained. The witch is an enduring symbol of power, independence, resistance and defiance, as she remains strong and proud of her lineage. She is simultaneously political, spiritual and magical and reclaims women's wisdom through herbal and medical lore associated with nature. Feminists reclaimed her in the form of feminist Wicca through participation in women's spiritual rituals, some from the past, and others recreated for the present.

Not all witchcraft is Goddess-centred, and not all Goddess spirituality features witchcraft, yet there remains a strong connection between the two. In a patriarchal society there are insufficient positive images of female power. Wicca has existed in every culture and country, even when hidden because of persecution. Wicca as a movement became established and more public in the UK in the 1950s. Doreen Valiente, a high priestess, founded her own coven in 1957 and wrote her 'Charge of the Goddess'.[4] Wicca practice was made legal in the UK in 1951 and was reclaimed, across the world. I really recommend Liz Williams' new book, *Miracles of Our Own Making: A History of Paganism* (2020), which gives a comprehensive history of paganism and of witchcraft. She is a powerful advocate of witchcraft in the world today.

Starhawk

The incredible and pioneering Starhawk bridges the worlds of Wicca and Goddess spirituality. She sees any perceived spiritual–political dichotomy as a middle-class, Western notion because in many cultures, particularly indigenous and Eastern ones, magic, spirituality and politics are not separate.

In the Wicca movement, Starhawk restored women's activism, creating sacred places and ritual practices to re-enchant the world. She rejected a polarised vision of women and men. For her, it is patriarchal cultures that divide, through unnecessary binary categories. Starhawk's work has continuously advocated for an engaged, political activist Goddess spirituality and for a revival of earth-based spirituality through her worldwide Reclaiming Movement. She wrote *The Empowerment Manual: A Guide for Collaborative Groups* (2011), in which she explored being leaderless or leaderful. She is the author of 13 books on an eclectic mix of feminism, earth-based spirituality, fiction, activism, Wicca, Goddess and leadership. I really recommend you explore her work, especially *The Spiral Dance: A Rebirth of the Ancient Religion of the Great Goddess* (1979), *The Earth Path: Grounding Your Spirit in the Rhythms of Nature* (2006) and *Truth or Dare: Encounters with Power, Authority and Mystery* (1991).

Audre Lorde

As a poet myself, I have been deeply moved by Audre Lorde, a black, lesbian writer and poet whose poetry and prose explored how all women, especially black women, are silenced by patriarchy's denial of their authentic existence. She encouraged women to reclaim the power of speech, to reject patriarchal names and to define reality for themselves. Silence, the absence of language and the transformation of silence are recurring themes throughout her work.

She turned to African Goddesses to reclaim the tradition of ancestors and to discard patriarchal religious beliefs and behaviours that oppress and disempower black people. In *Zami: A New Spelling of My Name* (1982), Lorde honoured all the women in her life who enabled her to name herself.

In *The Black Unicorn: Poems* (1995 edition), she turns to the pantheon of African Gods and Goddesses and creates the female Afrekete. She explores how black women find spirituality through travelling to the deep core of their ancestral roots and reclaiming their true souls. She consistently challenges her black readers to overcome internalised whiteness and to affirm their own worth and self-love. For Lorde, the black Goddess symbolises that which is dark and ancient and Divine in all women, affirming that black women are physically, emotionally and spiritually Divine. She provides, for women of all races, powerful and liberating images of female wisdom and strength.

Monica Sjöö

Monica Sjöö was a Swedish painter, writer and radical anarchist feminist and ecofeminist who lived and worked in the UK. Her most famous painting is the controversial *God Giving Birth*, depicting a woman giving birth. This painting represents her perception of the Great Mother as the universal creator of cosmic life.

Sjöö and Barbara Mor co-authored *The Great Cosmic Mother: Rediscovering the Religion of the Earth* (1987), one of the first books to uncover the hidden history of the Goddess and to propose that humanity's earliest religious and cultural belief systems were created and first practised by women. It has influenced many women's studies, mythology and religious courses since 1968. Her ideological leadership and way of working offered an early example of intersectional politics woven into Goddess spirituality.

Her later work, *Return of the Dark/Light Mother or New Age Armageddon: Towards a Feminist Vision of the Future* (1999), is one of my favourite books. It is simultaneously a memoir in which she processes the deaths of her two sons, a feminist polemic, a celebration of Goddess, an Earth manifesto, a description of her mystical experiences at sacred sites and an apocalyptic warning about the dangers of new age ideology. These prophetic words of hers deeply resonate with me: "Now is the time for all visionaries to come to the aid of our ancient Earth Mother.

We must struggle to make far-reaching changes politically and economically if we are to survive."(1999, p298)

Ecofeminism

Ecofeminism sees a profound connection between the exploitation and degradation of the natural world and the subordination and oppression of women. It emerged in the mid-1970s and is both a movement and a philosophy. It exposes the oppression of women and the environment as interlinked and rooted in patriarchal structures. From a pantheistic and pagan view, Goddess is experienced and embodied in nature and the land. The rhythms of Goddess and nature are one, manifested through the birth–death–rebirth cycle, closely associated with the biological embodiment of the female. She is also Gaia, the cosmos, the web of life, the matrix. In this view, Goddess does not transcend the world: She manifests in and through us; we are Her embodiment, whatever our gender. Goddess spirituality has also awakened women's political agency in ecology and social movements aimed at resacralising the relationship between nature and humans.

Ecospirituality has expressed itself in protests against nuclear power, fossil energy, fracking, climate change and extinction, driven by a desire to save Mother Earth and protect her from unrelenting damage and exploitation. In *Ecofeminism: Women, Animals, Nature* (1993), Greta Gaard edits a fascinating dialogue among feminists, ecofeminists, animal liberationists, deep ecologists and social ecologists in an effort to create a sustainable lifestyle for all inhabitants of the earth. Among the issues addressed are conflicts between green politics and ecofeminism, applications of ecofeminism, harmful implications of the romanticised woman–nature association in Western culture and cultural limitations of ecofeminism. Two books my students have really enjoyed, as have I, are by Sharon Blackie: *If Women Rose Rooted: A Life-Changing Journey to Authenticity and*

Belonging (2016) and *The Enchanted Life: Unlocking the Magic of the Everyday* (2018).

Women's Spirituality Reformists

Among the women who created a spiritual–political path with female rather than male divinities was ecofeminist, ethicist and thealogian Mary Daly. In *Beyond God the Father: Toward a Philosophy of Women's Liberation* (1973), she analysed how patriarchal religions destroyed matricentric cultures. She was highly influential in moving the religious discourse beyond religious understanding of God as the father. Daly introduced the notion of Goddess as verb rather than noun. She called for women to 'exodus' from patriarchal religions and their consistent and deliberate exclusion and subordination of women which denied them the full actualisation of their unique spiritual expression.

Two new feminist traditions then arose: first, the women who stayed within a patriarchal religion to reclaim the sacred feminine and imagine divinity as female from within; and second, those who went outside to form an active Goddess spirituality separate from, and in direct challenge to, all forms of patriarchal religions.

The women who stayed were termed the 'reformists'. They disputed claims by men that God is beyond identification with either the male or female sex on the basis that the common and accepted usage of male language conveys a clear message that God is male. They brought attention to the fact that the religious world is designed by men's imagination and needs with a male God functioning as the primary and only ultimate point of reference for understanding spiritual experience, life and the world. They also recognised that their faith traditions had also spiritually sustained generations of foremothers and foresisters in the faith.

These reformist women have contributed beautiful and

powerful work to introduce female or non-sexist language in liturgy and songs. They have created female imagery, written *The Woman's Bible*, reclaimed women within holy scriptures and fought for women clergy on an equal footing with men as ordained ministers where these were not allowed. The reformists argued that using female images challenges the literal-mindedness of the male images in God-talk and opens new conversations about holy mystery. Their aim was to realise coequal human and spiritual dignity with men.

I have trained as an interfaith minister and have journeyed experientially with many different traditions, particularly Buddhism and Christianity, in depth over many years. For me, most faith traditions reflect our societal patriarchy with male power and hierarchy dominating and continuing the oppression and subjugation of women, with only minor changes, which are tokenism.

The Abrahamic faiths of Christianity, Islam and Judaism still consider women inferior, unclean and sinful temptresses. Theravada Buddhism, which I participated in for 12 years, is rigidly hierarchical on gender lines. Hinduism, Islam and Catholicism do not allow females to be in formal liturgical or leadership roles. Liberal Judaism does have female rabbis, yet practices such as separating the sexes and praying about being glad not to be born a woman are still prevalent. The Protestant Christian and Zen Buddhism traditions have been more accepting of women in formal ministerial roles. Female gurus in Hinduism and Buddhism have established independent ashrams or sanghas. Brahma Kumaris, founded in India in 1937, by a man, allows only female leaders, known as 'Dadis' (senior sisters). The equality of men and women is a fundamental principle of the Bahá'í faith, yet women may not serve as members of the Universal House of Justice, its highest governing body.

Thealogy

> God may be in the details, but Goddess is in the question.
> **Gloria Steinem** (1994, p. 270)

The term 'thealogy' is created from 'thea', the Greek word for Goddess. Thealogy attempts to articulate in a cohesive and understandable way how Goddess is experienced. It emerged in the 1970s as a counterpoint to 'theology'. Today, thealogy is an extensively studied topic, also known as Goddess Feminism. Some of the main thealogy writers are Carol P. Christ, Mary Daly, Naomi Goldenberg, Judith Plaistow, Melissa Raphael and Rosemary Radford Ruether.

Initially it was felt that thealogy might create disembodied, elitist knowledge and intellectual understanding characteristic of patriarchal scholarship. Fortunately, the women involved created a very different experiential and embodied perspective on spirituality. Thealogy became useful for women to help them make sense of their own distinctive experiences. It also brought Goddess spirituality into academia, giving it intellectual integrity, respectability and acceptance as a valid arena of discourse and research. All the writers I mention above are well worth reading. If thealogy interests you, you are in for a treat; it absolutely fascinates me. As it's such an extensive topic, I will focus on just one thealogian and her work.

Carol P. Christ

Carol P. Christ's *Rebirth of the Goddess: Finding Meaning in Feminist Spirituality* (1997) and *She Who Changes: Reimagining the Divine in the World* (2003) are powerful expressions of a systematic thealogy. She articulates how the female imagery and symbolism of Goddess represents and legitimates the women's movement, much as God symbolism in Christianity upholds and reinforces the interests of men in patriarchy.

For Christ, women's spirituality is strongly connected to an awareness of life's complex interconnectedness and to a feminist spirituality that is ecologically centred. Rejecting dualisms and hierarchies, she believes in the unity of all beings in harmony with nature. Goddess as understood only through a transcendental and superior form through contemplation or revealed scriptures is not enough. She explores how women's spirituality typically begins from experience, rather than from theory. She articulates the gender difference in women's religious experience and how women have holistic, discursive, emergent and concrete views of the world, very different from linear, sequential, reductionist and abstract thinking.

She is clear that every individual has the potential for many ways of experiencing the Divine, but that patriarchal religions don't allow for women's ways of spiritual experience or expression. She has produced eight books on women and religion and wrote a highly significant essay in 1978 which is still relevant: 'Why Women Need the Goddess'.[5] I recommend that you read this essay and, if it inspires you, do explore more of her work. She has hugely influenced me as we share a panentheistic view of Goddess.

Goddess Mythology

Mythos is a system of symbols and rituals which help meaning-making by providing a sense of what is important, real and true. It can also offer and establish patterns of action. At the heart of Goddess mythos is the experience and insight that Goddess is nature, the land and embodied, and that everything in the web of life is connected and interconnected. As patriarchal mythos is one of domination and separation, many women have turned to exploring and transforming themselves and the prevalent cultural mythos by subverting old myths and creating new ones. This involves working with myths, fairy tales, sacred texts and stories; revising or rewriting old texts to create new understandings and perspectives; creating new myths and cosmologies or retelling stories from the perspectives of the main female characters. This tradition also includes sacred drama, performing with masks or dancing ancient and modern myths and fables. There are a plethora of modern novels being published within this tradition as well as numerous academic papers. These help us to challenge, re-envision and resist patriarchy.

Kathy Jones

Kathy Jones has made a huge contribution to modern Goddess spirituality. She is a visionary, pioneer, writer, healer, sacred dramatist and founder of the Lady of Avalon Goddess tradition. She also set up the first licensed Goddess Temple, in modern times, as a place of worship and legal handfasts in Glastonbury. She has established a wide range of priestess and priest training and other related Goddess Temple programmes. The community holds regular Goddess ceremonies and an annual Glastonbury Goddess Conference, which Kathy founded. She has also established a Goddess Hall and a Goddess House: gorgeous spaces for education and healing activities. She has developed the MotherWorld vision and, more recently, the MotherWorld political party.

She has written five inspiring books about different aspects of the Avalonian Goddess path and gives talks, training courses and keynotes all over the world. I am fortunate to have inspiring personal conversations with Kathy, which challenge and nourish my understanding of Goddess. As I say in the acknowledgements, she is the spark that lit my Luminary flames and encouraged me to birth the Luminary Wheel. I encourage you to read all her books, including the most influential: *Priestess of Avalon, Priestess of the Goddess: A Renewed Spiritual Path for the 21st Century*.

Modern Goddess Temples and Communities

New temples and communities dedicated to Goddess are being established all over the world, including in Australia, the USA, the UK and Europe. Goddess temples have always existed in some parts of the world, especially Africa, Egypt, Greece and India. It is well worth searching online to see whether there is a Goddess temple and community near you.

* * *

I would like also to mention a man's journey to Goddess as articulated by Tim Ward, in his compelling personal account of his experiences with Goddess in *Savage Breast: A Man's Search for the Goddess*. My male students have found this journey valuable and encouraging.

* * *

I hope you have enjoyed this brief exploration of Goddess spirituality and its place in the world today. It may be familiar to some of you, for others a whole new topic. My purpose in sharing this is to help you feel better informed of the underpinning as you travel through my Goddess Luminary Leadership Wheel.

Chapter 2

A New Way

The Luminary training has been a golden gift that keeps giving. Lynne is a rare and exceptional teacher, bringing an atmosphere of respect, inclusivity and compassion to her work. Her work is firmly framed by an academic rigour and underpinned by strong and open-minded spiritual roots. It makes for an excellent learning environment. Students are encouraged in a generous and illuminated way. In my lifetime of retreats, courses and training courses, this one stood out for all the right reasons. It was wonderful to have my leadership experiences witnessed and understood in the contemporary context. The Luminary training became a rite-of-passage for me into a mature and confident leadership. A sloughing-off of outmoded assumptions and a personal reclamation of rights and space.

Tania, Goddess Luminary

Introduction

Nolava (Avalonian Goddess) continuously gives birth to

the new in all forms. From Her deep bottomless Womb, She creates new ways of being, new ideas and thoughtforms, both personal and communal, that come into existence. **Kathy Jones** (2006, p. 226)

In this chapter I discuss the Goddess Luminary Leadership Wheel within the current societal context and explore the different paradigms and perspectives of leadership over time. I challenge the value of conventional stereotypes of the feminine and masculine and the current paradigms from which most leadership has originated. I conclude with a description of feminism, feminist leadership and my views on gender. I offer leadership development from a very different leadership source, world view and identity from conventional models. My approach is explicitly female and feminist, as well as spiritual. Gender is the most significant predictor of poverty and powerlessness, and gender inequality remains a pervasive and fundamental obstacle to human development and the guarantee of universal human rights.

Societal Context

The Challenges

We live in a complex and highly challenging world. Issues such as climate change, financial crises, the rise of nationalism, the expansion of social media and the ever-increasing pace and demands of daily life are all changing the way we live, feel and behave. Levels of stress and behavioural and mental health problems are rising significantly. Several polls and research findings indicate that some people today are experiencing a range of types of crisis and are looking for meaning and purpose. Concerns are manifesting as anxiety, depression, wanting to change lifestyles or downsizing. Young people have limited opportunities to find work, unemployment is high, and the homeless are living on the streets or in cramped or unaffordable spaces.

Too many people feel that their workplaces are uninspired, and they bring their bodies but not their whole selves to work. People are tired of unproductive meetings, infighting, bureaucracy, corruption, being overworked and overwhelmed: all the things that restrict and disempower them. People who find meaning, in and through their paid work, often feel more fulfilled. I have explored bringing your whole self into your workplace for many years in my quest to co-create healthy and high-spirited work communities in further education.

The demands facing humanity, especially women, can seem overwhelming. The acute need to deal with climate change, biodiversity, extinction and horrific abuses of human rights is obvious. In the current patriarchal system, the oppression of women and the limitations placed on them continues. The incompetence of patriarchy and capitalism to solve critical issues is being highlighted by new generations yearning for a better world. The rise in nationalism and extremisms is turning back much of the progress towards social justice made in previous decades.

Women and Covid

The Covid pandemic is exacerbating some of the most insidious and pervasive inequities women have ever faced. The economic and physical disruptions caused by the pandemic have negative consequences for the rights and health of women and girls in every country. The gains made for women in the past decades are at risk of being rolled back. The pandemic is deepening pre-existing inequalities, exposing vulnerabilities in social, political and economic systems. The impacts of Covid are exacerbated for women and girls simply by virtue of their sex across every sphere, including health, the economy, security and social protection. Throughout the pandemic, women have consistently raised concerns that they are more likely to be furloughed and more likely to be doing home schooling, low-wage work, raising a child on their own or doing unpaid work as caregivers. Women have lost their jobs at a higher rate than men since the onset of the pandemic. Women will be less likely than men to return to paid employment.

According to a United Nations Population Fund (UNFPA) report (April 2020), months of sustained global lockdown will leave 47 million women in low- and middle-income countries unable to use modern contraceptives, leading to a projected 7 million additional unintended pregnancies.[6]

There are millions of additional cases of gender-based violence in domestic and public spaces and significant delays in programmes to end female genital mutilation and child marriage. Medical experts warn regularly that the pandemic will set women back decades and increase the gender pay gap because of balancing work and childcare.

One of the clearest ways in which systematic oppressions have been revealed is through the treatment and reality of working life for frontline workers, especially nurses; these are mostly women who are undervalued and underpaid. Domestic violence has escalated, and shelters have closed due to lack of funds, resulting in far fewer places people can go to for support.

ActionAid undertook a rapid assessment of the impact of Covid on young women in India, Ghana, Kenya and South Africa. Its report (ActionAid, 2020) illustrates how the global pandemic exposes and exacerbates pre-existing crises, with young people being hit especially hard. It urges governments to reject failed policy templates and development models and urgently replace them with policies and actions specifically aimed at permanently removing pervasive inequalities for young women in low-income households who continue to be excluded in multiple ways.[7]

According to Rosa, a charity that funds grassroots women's organisations, women's jobs are 1.8 times more vulnerable to the pandemic than men's.[8] The National Domestic Abuse line has seen a 25 per cent increase in demand. Lockdown measures have contributed to isolation and mental health distress. Black and minority women have been particularly exposed to the impacts of the pandemic, which continues to cause harm more fiercely along racial lines. As we recover and rebuild after the pandemic, I pray that we will seize the opportunity to transform economic systems that discriminate against women and all disadvantaged groups.

The Solutions

On a more positive note, women around the world are rising, resisting and voicing their numerous concerns, as shown by a tsunami of feminist protests, campaigns and online activism. New eco-movements and black-led movements for racial justice are bringing renewed attention to the threats and realities of violence, extinction, continuing oppressions, injustices and greed. We are at a major transformative moment on several fronts, especially on race, women's issues, climate and extinction, as well as facing the urgent impact of Covid.

New forms of protest movement are gaining traction, and grassroots initiatives are making a difference. Grassroots movements in the USA, not grotesque sums spent on advertising, won the election for the Democrats. Leaders in modern social movements and feminist organisations focus on empowering the front line. Powerful multiracial, intergenerational coalitions are using anti-racist and feminist principles to mobilise transformative change, address the climate crisis and co-create a better society. Young and older activists, communities most at risk and those with the fewest resources, as well as progressive politicians and some public sector leaders, are generating more radical demands and are calling for transformative change.

Women are increasingly assuming leadership roles in social justice movements as new forms of feminism, the Black

Lives Matter movement and Extinction Rebellion respond to the injustices faced by particular groups of people. These movements are introducing new forms of leadership aimed at empowering individuals and communities and protecting those who are most vulnerable. I recommend exploring two interesting women, both co-founders of high-profile protest movements: Gail Bradbrook of Extinction Rebellion and Alicia Garza of Black Lives Matter. Garza's book, *The Purpose of Power*, is a significant contribution to new forms of Leaderful and collective ways of leading.

Women Leading Effectively in Crisis

All leadership is contextual. I have examined how elected female heads of state or government were successful in the face of the beginning of the Covid crisis. Many of the countries with the most effective responses early on were led by women. I have no doubt that at some point these women will be criticised, but I want to capture a significant moment for herstory of powerful women manifesting outstanding leadership.

Most lauded is the powerful and effective leadership of Jacinda Ardern in New Zealand, Angela Merkel in Germany, Sanna Marin in Finland, and Tsai Ing-wen in Taiwan. Of course, male leaders in some countries have also led in effective ways throughout the pandemic, but many have led disastrously. In my view, the most effective Covid leaders have exhibited a mix of masculine and feminine characteristics as well as being authentic, skilful and appropriate to their context.

From my reading and analysis, I have identified certain characteristics.

The female leaders remained present, calm, authentic and clear throughout. They faced difficult truths about the forthcoming pandemic early on and didn't shy away from its magnitude or disastrous impact. They engaged through meaning-making and encouragement rather than fear or compliance. When needed they did whatever was necessary to create safety. They exhibited high emotional intelligence by acknowledging the deep suffering that people were experiencing and the tragedy that was unfolding.

In their communications, interactions and speeches they showed genuine empathy, emotion and care without being overwhelmed or people losing confidence in their ability to act. They were not condescending to those who were confused, resistant, angry or frightened. They communicated effectively through social media with regular updates, supported by the experts. They took decisive and difficult decisions when needed, never shying away from what they believed was right. Ardern brought in the army when the system she had put in place failed to work in the quarantine centres. They didn't play aggrandisement games or make the overreaching, unfulfilled claims made elsewhere by male leaders. They took full responsibility for everything that happened in their respective countries – the successes and the mistakes – without blaming anyone else. They relied on the science, listened to the experts and responded to what the experts were telling them.

I believe these female leaders saw the pandemic crisis as an interconnected, whole-system problem with different parts of their national system needing to work together to co-create new solutions. They were early adapters unashamedly learning in the midst of the crisis. People saw their genuine humanity, professionalism and competence shine through. They built trust and were perceived as trustworthy. In other countries, trust was clearly a problem and messages kept changing, whereas these women gave consistent messages and explained thoroughly why and when something changed.

Perspectives of Leadership

In these complex, turbulent and challenging times, leaders need to be as expansive, authentic and adaptable as possible. In this multi-perspective world, it becomes important to know your own world view and beliefs as well as remaining open, responsive to and aware of perspectives different from yours. Over the past 40 years, I have explored and experimented with a wide range of leadership perspectives. Having worked as a chief executive of a leadership centre that supported and worked directly with 40,000 people in leadership positions, I understand that anyone's leadership experience and journey happens within one or more of the different perspectives of leadership, depending upon their unique context, world view and self-awareness. You can travel through many different perspectives, as I have done, or remain within one you feel comfortable in. Mainstream leadership theory was shaped within a gendered system all over the world.

One of my reasons for developing the Goddess Luminary Leadership Wheel teachings was my experience in further education, and elsewhere, of people of colour, women, working-class people, anyone with a disability and others from marginalised groups who felt that leadership was not for them because of its association with individualism, white male hero stereotypes or charismatic leadership. None of these fitted with their own sense of who they were, and wanted to be, in the world. They often felt leadership was not for them. One of the most touching moments of my life is when I did a talk on my leadership style to a group of people of colour on an aspiring college leadership course in 1999. Here is some feedback I received:

> *Lynne, this is the first time I've ever heard anyone speak about leadership in a way that I can relate to. You have just illustrated for me a way in which I can be a leader without selling my soul. A way I didn't know was possible before listening to you.*

This was the moment I decided that leadership development could be one of the ways I could contribute as part of my professional life and to social justice more broadly. I felt inspired to challenge the prevailing perspectives.

We all have an image in our head of what a leader looks and sounds like; for too long that image has been white and male. Changing our internalised images takes deliberate effort and may need support. Over time, notions of what makes a good leader have shifted, and there are now many different ones available.

I developed the table below to explore and clarify a chronological shift in perspectives from the 1920s to recent times within modern, primarily Western, leadership theory and practice. This is my context, so the table is a personal mapping of my unique journey.

Management	operational, strategic
Traits	personality, heroic, style, position
Excellence	quality processes, standards
Visionary	charismatic, purpose, mission
Culture	diversity, trust, context, learning
Values	character, inner life, trust
Servant	humility, service, stewardship
Feminist	gender justice, patriarchy, power, leaderless
Followers	distributed, collective
Systems	cross boundaries, seeing the whole context
Sustainability	ecosystems, social responsibility
Adaptive	multiple perspectives, complexity
Entrepreneurial	self-sustaining, enterprising
Virtues	wisdom, ethics, philosophy, character
Eastern or African	philosophies and approaches
Teal	wholeness, self-management, evolutionary purpose
Spiritual	source, state of being, presence
Goddess	Goddess Gnosis, cyclical, elemental

From the top, the leadership perspectives move from being about answers, and individualism, with rules and control, down the table, to leadership of empowerment, innovation and a collective and emergent phenomenon. Another way of seeing the shift – from top to bottom – is from the scientific and linear focus, the cult of personality and transactional exchange to leadership that is transformational, spiritual and holistic.

It is important to recognise that the lens through which most mainstream leadership approaches are understood is that of a privileged white male, which excludes individuals from non-dominant identities, including women. In some ways, leadership thinking and development has travelled a long way from the 'great man' traits of the late nineteenth century. It has incorporated emotional intelligence, female qualities, eco, values, vision, soul and spirituality influences. Yet none of these important influences explicitly challenge the patriarchal paradigm, and too many organisations are still functioning with heroic, charismatic or individualistic leadership models. Leadership literature is still dominated by male writers, and most leadership constructs are white, male heteronormative and Western-centric. As a mainstream leader in further education, as well as exploring and experimenting with conventional approaches, I have studied leadership steeped in ubuntu (which has roots in humanist African philosophy), Islam, Hinduism, the Tao-Te-Ching, Buddhism, indigenous wisdom, paganism and Zen.

Challenges to patriarchal leadership have been made by feminists and emerging social protest movements and by post-conventional and Teal practices (explored more fully in my monograph, *The Luminary Leaderful Way: Goddess Luminary Wheel Teachings* (2019),[9] and in the Spiral 2 course).

Goddess Luminary Leadership Wheel is influenced by and infused with feminist, Leaderful, Teal, post-conventional, integral, spiritual, soulful, embodiment, adaptive, activist and modern protest perspectives as well as incorporating the best aspects of conventional leadership. The eclectic range of leadership writers by whom I have been profoundly influenced include Srilatha Batliwala, adrienne maree brown, Jody Fry, Peter Hawkins, Giles Hutchins, Frederick Laloux, Judi Neal, Peter Senge, Otto Scharmer, Starhawk, William Torbert, Simon Western and Margaret Wheatley. There are many others, some named throughout this book.

Exercise

1. You may want to reflect on your leadership journey to date.
2. Which of these perspectives have you had experience of?
3. How did that approach work, or not, for you?
4. Which perspective(s) are you currently in?
5. You may want to create your own list of perspectives to articulate your experiences.

Challenging Conventional Stereotypes

We must reject not only the stereotypes that others have of us but also those that we have of ourselves.
Shirley Chisholm (Winslow, 2013)

I feel strongly that conventional male-centred, patriarchal leadership paradigms have failed women and continue to do so. I have spent my life simultaneously working within and challenging patriarchal conventions. It's what I do as an edge-walker and a change agent. I challenge the conventional in three ways:

- first, by offering the Goddess Luminary Wheel as a radical alternative leadership programme
- second, by integrating feminist leadership principles
- third, through embracing a more fluid, gender-expansive way of articulating Goddess spirituality.

I focus less on the differences and more on developing, enhancing, encouraging and fostering the fullest potential of every person, regardless of any gender binary or societal limitations.

Issues of being a woman and a leader have mattered to me, as a female senior leader in further education from the age of 30, every day in my working life. It's been both a blessing and a burden. To help me on my journey of understanding, I have extensively studied and explored the female perspective and contribution within modern leadership theory and practice.

I understand the trajectory and importance of bringing the feminine, or sacred feminine, into leadership as a counterpoint to charismatic, heroic, male, individualistic and dominator leadership. I welcome cultivating an integrated balance of stereotypical feminine and masculine qualities according to need and context. This approach has been richly explored and practised for a long time. In my view, it has severe limitations. The best that can be achieved in this paradigm is the goal of women being different from and equally important to men, as it fosters the continuation of binary thinking and solutions that don't challenge or work to remove patriarchy and institutionalised sexism. It also falls into an essentialist view that certain categories, including women, have an underlying reality or true nature and a set of attributes that are necessary to their identity and function. While I believe that essentialism is an inevitable feature of the way most human beings think in the world today, I would like to see more conscious and inclusive ways of understanding the identities of women.

Angela Saini (2018) provides a detailed examination of the science that underpins our understanding of gender and the inferiority of women in society. She evidences the bias of science, conflicting research findings and the contribution of feminists and queer researchers. She argues that science does not prove that one sex is inferior and the other superior, and concludes that we already have everything we need for society to treat everyone as equals.

Bringing feminine qualities into male-centred leadership involves a perspective based on the binary view that women and men are very different. Patriarchy thrives on duality and opposites. We are born into a polarised society in which gender is characterised in a way that favours the masculine and diminishes the feminine. Masculinity has been intertwined with dominance, power and control. Femininity has been aligned with characteristics such as frailty, caring, gentleness and so forth. Society has created a distorted definition of gender, encouraging the belief that masculine and feminine characteristics are different, and at best complementary.

I believe that gender and these stereotypes are socially constructed. I remember sharing an article with my colleagues in 1983 by Peter Drucker, a well-respected leadership writer, called 'The Future of Management is Female'. A common and well-known refrain these days but unheard of in the early 1980s. My male peers did not receive it well. Things have moved on drastically since then for the better, yet stereotypical myths still prevail.

There is a partial truth in the view that some male leaders tend to behave assertively, decisively, logically, and feel comfortable within dominator hierarchies of control and command. So too, some female leaders may prefer more collective, less hierarchical forms of leadership, and behave in egalitarian, intuitive and team-spirited ways. But not all can or do. Often, when examined more closely, women and men draw on a mix of so-called 'masculine' and 'feminine' characteristics. Inevitably, feminine leadership strengths have been less valued in organisations than the masculine strengths. Female leaders in organisations historically shaped by the model of the heroic leader often have a deeply uncomfortable journey through the leadership pipeline.

As a senior female leader, I was given the choice of emulating masculine characteristics rather than adopting more feminine approaches, which I preferred yet were less valued in the organisational culture. As a feminist, I was fortunate in that I understood what being a woman meant to me, and was aware of the systemic issues of power, so I chose to develop a leadership style in which I could be authentically Lynne, whatever that turned out to be. I learned how to play the organisational game, managing the dilemma of not being seen as too aggressive nor too pliable, or of being a pushover or overly emotional. Over many years, I learned how to express both male and female qualities, in an integrated way, as was appropriate to the situation. Not an easy journey, it required significant introspection, experimentation and making mistakes; often learning the hard way alongside significant breakthroughs and success.

I find it overly simplistic to believe that if we introduce all or some feminine qualities into leadership then everything can be transformed. In my view, leadership development programmes encouraging sacred feminine or feminine leadership from an essentialist perspective have value but also fall short in recognising the variety and complexity of women and men, as they rely on binary stereotyping.

Often, they also lack any analysis or understanding of the inherent power differentials based on societal and institutional sexism that disproportionately affect women in adverse ways. Although some sexism and structural barriers are no longer legal, they're still very much with us. A range of factors, such as unconscious bias and continuing adherence to male-informed models of leadership in organisations, are severely limiting attempts at change and equality. Biases and cultural norms that subordinate women are everywhere. Continuing to advance the rights and opportunities of women continues to be a crucial and high-priority action.

The focus on changing laws remains important, but it is also essential to transform centuries-old cultural norms, values and behaviours around women's roles, contribution, capabilities and value. People who may be genuinely and explicitly committed to egalitarianism still have gender biases, in certain contexts, and unconsciously concoct post hoc rationalisations for discriminating behaviour.

We need to deconstruct the Western, patriarchal definition of masculinity and femininity, not just accommodate it. It seems to me that both men and women possess characteristics of both the masculine and the feminine, so we don't need any separation or codification of two types of characteristics in this way. I see a spectrum on which men and women are in different places, depending as much on their unique combination of personality, talents, brains and societal context as they do on their biological sex. For me, a significant part of travelling beyond the two stereotypes was to reclaim my inner feminine and masculine into an integrative fullness of choice and possibilities beyond polarities, into an experience of wholeness and expansiveness.

Feminisms

Feminism is not dying. It's getting reinvented, it's getting revitalised and people are creating new spaces and new axes of organising.
Srilatha Batliwala (IWDA, 2019)

A common understanding of feminism is the theory, belief and aim of the political, economic, and social equality and liberation of women. I believe that feminism is for everyone: women, men and people of all gender identities. It is not about exclusion, aggression or one gender coming out on top. Our understanding of gender has undergone significant change since the early days of organised feminism. For me, feminism is all about ending sexism, abolishing patriarchy and fighting against the oppression of women and all forms of sexist exploitation. I also believe that capitalism holds patriarchy in place and will continue to do so.

For many women, Goddess spirituality is intertwined with a feminist perspective, and their personal spirituality may feel highly political and an important motivator for change and for women's empowerment. For others, feminism doesn't feel relevant, so please take from my teaching only what interests you and feels valuable. This section may inspire you or it may feel irrelevant. Either is fine: it's your choice. You may choose to go straight to Chapter 3.

Feminism has existed ever since protests about the oppression of women have been made, initially by individual women from all over the world. Many amazing women, not recorded for herstory, have done magnificent things on behalf of other women. There were many individual women who campaigned and spoke out against the oppression of women from very early times. Feminism is not an invention of women in the West: it has existed in all cultures all over the world. Women are not a homogeneous group; there are numerous forms and perspectives of feminism with many faces and many forms, so it's more accurate to talk about feminisms.

To understand feminisms, we need to understand two central terms: patriarchy and intersectionality.

Patriarchy was the original institutionalised system of oppression that gave birth to the rest, an encompassing force of oppression and inequality. Feminism holds the view and central position that patriarchy is a political, social and mental system that perpetuates the myth that men should be dominant purely because they are born male. Patriarchy is gender-based systematic oppression through which bias, discrimination and power collude to create systems that exclude women and express misogyny as a strategy to accumulate and maintain power. It reinforces the gender stereotypes of male and female, based on male superiority and power and women's inferiority and weakness. Patriarchy also limits and censors men's emotional expression by not allowing them to express all aspects of themselves and fostering male identity based on a toxic, patriarchal masculinity. At worst, patriarchy deliberately oppresses and excludes many groups, which become othered. Patriarchy is not just a women's issue. Some feminist analyses place capitalism as the more central oppression.

* * *

Intersectionality explores our 'intersections' in terms of our lived experience of discrimination and oppression. Kimberlé Crenshaw coined the term 'intersectionality' in her highly influential article in the *University of Chicago Legal Forum* (Crenshaw, 1989). She encouraged the understanding, already a lived experience but not clearly articulated, that no axis of identity can be understood as separable from others to fight patriarchy. Each individual, and every social institution, is the site of multiple intersecting identities that afford privilege or oppression, or a mix of both. A group of individuals who share one identity or oppression, such as women sharing gender, may also experience life very differently, depending on their race. So, for example, white women and black women share gender experiences as women but have very different experiences with racism.

Everything that can marginalise people is considered important and relevant. This can include gender, race, class, sexual orientation, physical ability, accent, income, mental health, education, physical health, neurodiversity, age or anything else. Patriarchy impacts and oppresses every minority or disadvantaged group separately, so many social movements are raising awareness, fighting injustice and making change for specific groups. Intersectionality calls us to embrace the unifying of different groups' aims to ensure that every type of discrimination faced by anyone is named, seen and fought for. Living at the intersection and being a member of multiple minority groups means that societal bias and discrimination impacts every aspect of your life. Intersectional feminism places women who are the most marginalised by racism, classism, gender discrimination and other oppressive forces at the forefront.

Studies of matriarchal or gynocratic societies suggest different styles of woman-led leadership from those of male patriarchal styles. While there is so much beauty, inspiration and wisdom in this line of study, it may perpetuate gender essentialism in reclaiming a universal woman, and can perpetuate ethnic essentialism whereby white Western women use the term to encompass women globally in their own image, physically and ideologically. Intersectionality in feminist politics aims to unpack essentialism to understand what divides us before we can hope to unite us. Women in the global south cannot achieve collective empowerment unless and until all aspects of colonialism and neocolonialism are understood and eradicated. I don't feel equipped to talk in more detail on this topic in this book; I am exploring it to understand more fully.

Intersectionality applies to everyone and requires deep reflexivity and willingness to change, especially from the most privileged. Whiteness can be implicitly normative even when diversity is explicitly expressed as a value and intention. While exploring and understanding 'intrapersonal multiple identities' or 'intersecting identities' is important, so is facing, challenging and changing the systemic and structural priorities of intersectionality.

* * *

My Goddess spirituality is deeply intersectional and favours coalition politics and organising with other groups based on shared, but differing, experiences of oppression and privilege. Many Western Goddess spirituality communities are overwhelmingly, if not entirely, white, which makes attention to intersectionality important, especially working with and honouring indigenous and oppressed cultures without cultural appropriation. I want the elimination of all forms of hierarchy and all systems of domination and toxic power, and for the preciousness of all life to be honoured.

Intersectionality is very real for me as a feminist, spiritual, white, working-class and bisexual woman. Everyone has their own unique experiences of discrimination and oppression. As a fulltime activist during second-wave feminism, an educator and an ally, I have challenged all forms of societal oppression based on class, race, gender, faith tradition, physical and learning ability and sexual orientation. I continue to do so. I moved to a multiracial area in 1978 and worked in the three multiracial London boroughs of Hackney, Tower Hamlets and Croydon, as my connection with people of colour had been so limited.

I was a further education diversity champion and adviser on extremisms, as chief executive of the Centre for Excellence in Leadership, and worked with a black coach to help me understand my own racism and other unconscious bias. It was challenging and took serious commitment. Now, as an elder in my sixties, living in Glastonbury in the UK, a predominantly white space, I continue to fight all oppressions as best I can. I don't share this for recognition or gratitude, but purely because it is part of who I am, and because it matters to me.

As the daughter of a mother who worked in low-paid roles, for economic reasons, I know that the feminist fight for being liberated from the kitchen into work did not set working-class women free, in the same way as it did middle-class women. The exploitation and brutalisation of women remains in all aspects of society, and I feel that liberating women needs to remain a central and significant focus. I also share the view that we cannot resolve or smash patriarchy without attention to all oppressions.

* * *

That women are treated unjustly and are oppressed by sexism is the reason that feminism began to form as an organised protest and campaigning movement to fight for political, economic and social equality for all women and for their liberation. One way of looking at feminist history and how it became an organised national and global movement worldwide is through the four waves of feminisms.

With renewed interest and participation in feminism, exciting new books are being published. Four recent books on the history and core premise of feminisms are:

- *Feminism is for Everybody: Passionate Politics* (hooks, 2000)
- *Feminisms: A Global History* (Delap, 2020)
- *Living a Feminist Life* (Ahmed, 2017)
- *The Futures of Feminism* (Bryson, 2021).

As a lifelong feminist, I have witnessed and lived through second-, third- and fourth-wave feminisms. Key questions for every wave, for every individual woman, and for anyone who identifies as feminist, are "What is each feminist or wave of feminism fighting for or against?" and "What am I fighting for or against?" The first wave, during the nineteenth and early twentieth centuries, focused on suffrage and women's right to vote. The second-wave liberation movement started in the early 1960s and lasted for about two decades. It was followed by the third and fourth waves from the 1990s onwards. All these waves have involved specific organised protests and campaigns on behalf of women and other oppressed groups.

The first wave was led primarily by white, middle-class women, within the lens of patriarchy. The second-wave feminist understanding of patriarchy focused more broadly yet was still primarily the domain of the perspectives and needs of white, middle-class women. Class, race and sexuality were significant for many women, but at times were ignored or had to be suppressed, to meet the greater need of the universal sisterhood. Feminism has expanded to include, and go beyond, the narrative of universal sisterhood to include all genders.

Third- and fourth-wave feminist understandings of patriarchy are broader as they attempt to capture the nuances of all oppressions. Younger feminists are much clearer in articulating how patriarchy doesn't express itself uniformly and cannot be understood independently of other systems of oppression. Today's feminism includes lived experience of and strong support for intersectionality and fights for the liberation of all oppressed groups.

A new wave of women are protesting all around the world; young and older women are stepping up in all forms of successful activism. There are many awe-inspiring stories of women such as Malala Yousafzai, Amika George, Stella Nyanzi, Autumn Peltier and many others, not to mention the Millions March, #MeToo, Everyday Sexism Project and TIME'S UP movements. These are unprecedented times, and we are witnessing a mass call for change in gender inequality and a new rise in feminism in women of all ages, in most countries. There are many, many ways to be feminist. For some of you, feminism will be an important ingredient to create your own unique flavour of being a Luminary and being Leaderful in the world. For others, this may not be important or relevant. For me, it's essential.

Reflection

1. To help you articulate your own personal feminism I suggest you think about three questions:
    *   What is your understanding and definition of feminism?
    *   What does it mean for you?
    *   Who do you believe feminism is for?
2. Really feel into your responses. Write them down. There are no right or wrong answers; you're just finding your own truth and clarity.
3. Can you articulate your own feminist values?
4. What will it involve for you to live by these values?

Feminist Leadership

Leadership from a feminist standpoint is informed by the power of the feminist lens, which enables the feminist leader to identify injustices and oppressions and inspires her to facilitate the development of more inclusive, holistic communities. Feminist leaders are motivated by fairness, justice, and equity and strive to keep issues of gender, race, social class, sexual orientation, and ability at the forefront.
Tracy R. Barton (2006, p. 238)

A core purpose of feminist leadership is to achieve gender justice. It also recognises the centrality of power and systemic oppression, as well as the personal and psychological aspects of leadership. Feminist leaders pay attention to, are aware of and address as best they can the historical and contemporary circumstances that have created power inequalities and oppression for women and other underrepresented groups. They actively work for social justice, empowerment, cooperation and the explicit redistribution of power and responsibility. They have a genuine desire to bring marginalised voices to the centre of the conversation.

Feminist leaders work collectively to overtly and consciously ensure that no one, regardless of race, class, gender, sexual orientation, religion or physical and mental ability, is treated unfairly. They value community development and collaboration in which everyone's presence and participation is valued. They are willing to undergo a process of personal self-awareness, transformation and consciousness-raising, and they study the context and history of feminism. At its heart, for me, feminist leadership is love in action, which develops the fullest potential of everyone.

Feminism has frequently explored alternatives to traditional oppressive, white, male ways of leading. I was involved in feminist groups trying to lead more collectively with shared leadership, or of being leaderless, in the 1970s. An invaluable debate, stimulated by Jo Freeman's *The Tyranny of Structurelessness* (1984), explored how the denial of the existence of any form of leadership in groups can lead to other forms of tyranny.[10]

This is because in any collective a structure, formal or informal, always exists in some form; to pretend otherwise masks where power really lies. Her paper provides a clear rationale for the necessity of explicit transparent structures and processes that do not deny the importance of stepping into leadership. I have created a Luminary model of power in Cycle III and encourage you to go deep into your own understanding of, relationship with and skilful holding and flowing of your own power.

Writers on feminist leadership include Kami Anderson, Srilatha Batliwala, Jo Freeman and Joy Wiggins. In *Feminist Leadership for Social Transformation: Clearing the Conceptual Cloud*, her report for Creating Resources for Empowerment in Action (CREA), Batliwala (2010) provides an excellent overview and synthesis of feminist leadership and presents her 4P model of power, principles, politics and practices.[11] She understands feminist leadership, not just as a set of ideas about what is wrong with the world and what needs to change, but also as a way of looking at being a leader that takes into account the reality of a woman's place and oppression in society. Feminist leadership primarily draws on the perspective of transformative leadership. My contribution is to link post-conventional leadership explicitly to feminist leadership and to Goddess spirituality.

Feminist Leadership in Action

ActionAid has been commended for putting its feminist principles into successful action through its governance and whole organisation. In 2021, it won the Charity Governance Award in the Board Diversity and Inclusivity category. The judges said that ActionAid won "because they are aiming for a radical reconfiguring of governance. They demonstrate they are living their feminist values by being the change that they want to see in the world." Judges also praised ActionAid's "bold innovation" and "practical solutions" to overcome inclusion challenges. It appoints trustees from diverse backgrounds, but also makes sure those trustees actively influence policy. The board has pioneered an app that monitors the amount of time men and women speak during a meeting, to avoid male dominance. It has adopted 10 feminist leadership principles: self-awareness; self-care and caring for others; dismantling bias; inclusion; sharing power; responsible and transparent use of power; accountable collaboration; respectful feedback; courage; and zero tolerance.[12]

For decades, Oxfam has supported women's leadership and participation, from the grassroots to policymaking, despite its recent issues with sexual misconduct. It has worked to transform unequal and oppressive uses and systems of power, and to strengthen the organisational capacity of women's organisations with women's leadership. It places importance on the *how*, as well as on *what* it does. Its 11 feminist principles are: I share power; I challenge my behaviour; I support the feminist movement; nothing about us without us; feminism is for everyone; there is no justice without gender justice; I champion diversity; I value safety; I want a supportive environment; I believe in freedom of expression; and eliminate gender-based violence.[13]

Oxfam has also done pioneering work in embedding these principles into the living practice of its leaders and into all its systems and processes. This is articulated in a useful document.[14]

Caplor Horizons is another charity exploring how to live and embed explicit feminist leadership in its organisation. I have worked with the Caplor Horizons team to develop their journey. They have engaged in seminars to understand the context and history of feminism. They are discussing how they think the next wave of feminism might express itself, as well as how they can contribute to that next wave. The four co-directors are actively sharing power as a quartet and are exploring deeply their relationship with power as leaders, individually and collectively. They have a strong focus on social justice, as well as the practical and cultural aspects.

I have mapped the 21 principles of feminist leadership from ActionAid and Oxfam on to the Goddess Luminary Leadership Wheel teachings. All their principles are embraced within the Wheel dimensions, other than zero tolerance.

Another useful source for feminist leadership is the work of Fairshare and its *Feminist Leaders for Feminist Goals* toolkit.[15]

Reflection

1. Explore the work of ActionAid, Oxfam or Caplor

Horizons to bring feminist leadership alive for you. Consider the following:

- What might you draw on to help you to live feminist leadership in your context?
- Which principles really resonate with you? Can you articulate your feminist principles?
- How does feminism influence your flavour of Luminary leadership?
- How might you commit to living your feminist values within your leadership?

Gender

I want there to be a place in the world where people can engage in one another's differences in a way that is redemptive, full of hope and possibility.
bell hooks (2009, p. 153)

The Goddess Luminary Leadership Wheel has direct and visceral knowing of Goddess at the centre. So why 'Goddess' and not a neutral word such as 'Source' or 'the Divine'? Goddess brings me to a fuller experience of the Divine as Birther, from which everyone, and everything, is born. Goddess is a larger concept than God, holding *all* the qualities we consider as feminine or masculine. 'She' literally includes 'he' and goes beyond all duality and societal binary notions of gender. She loves all Her creation, everyone and everything She births. She holds the fullest potential of all that can be manifested, for everyone to be fully themselves.

To me, as a feminist in a patriarchal society, reclaiming Goddess and celebrating Her in an inclusive and expansive female form feels more powerful than a male or gender-neutral divinity. So, I place Goddess at the centre very consciously.

When choosing words for all the dimensions on the Wheel,

I have not used conventional binary gender terms as it felt that doing so would immediately spin the Wheel into a binary polarity. The words I use are gender neutral to encourage and allow for the fullest potential of anyone exploring the Wheel, whatever their gender identity.

Gender is complex. Women are not a homogeneous group. Race, disability, age, socio-economic situation and sexual orientation, as well as many other influences, all shape our gender identities and experiences. I agree with the view that gender is a social construct and that we are moulded by a wide range of social and peer influences as we grow into adulthood. These influences generate a conventional view, based on stereotypes, of how a girl and boy should behave. It is important to acknowledge the wounding and pain of anyone seen or treated as other, as outsider or not normative; alongside the support and healing they may need.

There are a wide range of conflicting views on gender. All over the world gender debates take place. It's a complex situation and the debates can become fierce.

At one end is overt discrimination and harmful rhetoric towards women, transgender and non-binary people. Many religions are averse to anything other than conventional binary perspectives. At the opposite end, trans activists advocate for the rights and acceptance of trans people and oppose all women-only spaces, which they feel exclude them. Gender inclusivity is challenging as it requires deep levels of self-reflection and sensitivities to views different from your own.

Some feminists and women within Goddess spirituality communities are gender critical and don't accept men transitioning as 'real' women. They cannot accept that trans women really understand how it is to be a true woman within patriarchy. Some Goddess communities struggle with different views over the inclusion of trans women in women's spaces and advocate trans-exclusionary practices because they feel the need to protect cis women-only spaces. I have read the work of gender-critical women, including the compendium of essays, *Female Erasure: What You Need to Know about Gender Politics' War on Women, the Female Sex and Human Rights*, edited by Ruth Barrett. This is a comprehensive compendium of views from women who feel they are being 'eroded' by the demands from trans women disrespecting the safety, needs or biological reality of cis women.

Goddess spirituality, as it developed in the 1970s and 1980s, was rooted in gender binary and gender essentialism. It is important to hear the views of Goddess women who feel strongly that a united, universal sisterhood has value, and inspires and nourishes them. Women are still oppressed as a group so it's important to continue to see women as a specifically oppressed group, with many aspects of their lives still requiring attention and liberation. It really matters to me to support all women and I respect the choice of those who want to focus purely on cis women's issues, while encouraging them to see any exclusive tendencies. Patriarchy oppresses all women purely based on their gender and this has been, and continues to be, my primary focus. I have experienced strong and beautiful universal sisterhood, as a second-wave feminist, and I also want a broader, intersectional and inclusive sisterhood to continue to express itself. As a feminist, it is vital for me to be part of making sure that all women can organise and fight against their oppression, while including all categories of women.

Intersectional feminists reject exclusionary narratives and work to support trans-rights and to protect all women, as defined in the broadest sense, from the negative impacts of patriarchy. Some intersectional feminists refuse to participate in Goddess activities or events that have trans-exclusionary statements or policies.

* * *

My preference, as an intersectional feminist, is to co-create spaces that allow for the authentic needs and empowerment and growth of everyone. I recognise the tensions and complexities of what this entails yet am committed to working together to move beyond the current differences. All perspectives of the gender conversations need to really listen to each other and to hear what each most values, beyond wounding and fear.

I am open to including trans women and non-binary people to share in the experience of Goddess blood mysteries and the magical, mystical way of the womb. I feel that the ultimate mystery lies with Goddess, not with each of us as individual women, and may or may not be reflected in our biology. Through Goddess rituals and mysteries, we are all nourished, interconnected, gestated and birthed. Mystery takes us beyond gender essentialism. It is not unusual for Goddess-loving women to genuinely be supportive and welcoming of individual transgender people and still feel they should be excluded from blood mysteries. I hold the view that Goddess wants any privileged or dominant group that holds power to be aware of any exclusion or discrimination, intentional or not. Being a feminist and a Goddess-loving person can manifest in numerous shapes and forms.

It has taken me significant work to understand and travel my own journey through gender, which I have undertaken willingly. My explorations have been helped by the writings of Susan Harper in 'The Future of Goddess' (2017) and of Julia Serano, especially *On the Outside Looking In* (2005).

I believe that the continuing unfolding of Goddess will question and eventually shift the current binary paradigm and gender tensions.

My path involves honouring Goddess spirituality as a radical, disruptive and significant act of revisioning and embodying the Divine, as female, within patriarchal society. It also involves actively encouraging, including and supporting

all non-normative, non-binary and transgender people drawn
to Goddess spirituality. Key to both is to explore, reveal and
challenge our participation in and maintenance of the gender
binaries of female and male, especially how we frame fixed
behaviours and expectations around these binaries. When
we open ourselves to an awareness of a more expansive
understanding and expression of gender, we make room to
challenge our own potentially harmful gender rigidity, and to
see what we are holding on to and still need within our own
gender identities. Doing this enables a whole new relationship
with anyone's female expression, internally and externally, as
well as assisting in healing all wounding. It also fosters sacred
embodiment and a deeper relationship with the land, nature
and cosmos.

* * *

My advice is to navigate the terrain and come to your own
view. I encourage everyone to find their fullest potential within
the Divine female of the Luminary Wheel journey, in the most
expansive and inclusive way possible, for them. May we each be
liberating and liberated in our Luminary Leaderfulness.

Reflection

1. Explore some or all of the questions below:
   - Are you clear and grounded in your own gender
     identity?
   - Have you studied and explored experiences from
     a range of different genders, particularly the non-
     binary or transgender perspective?
   - Do you understand your own internal response to
     and any reactivity regarding queer people?
   - How do you know your views and actions are

genuinely not transphobic or created out of fear?

- Have you worked out for yourself how you can balance your love and experience of Goddess with a genuine inclusiveness and embracing of queer?
- How can you ensure that cis women are honoured and respected in relation to important Goddess practices?
- If you are a trans person, how are you understanding and honouring issues important to cis women?
- Where do you personally set boundaries of safety and inclusion for specific interest groups without being exclusionary?
- Is it possible for you to get to know some non-binary or transgender people personally? If not, read some of the moving and powerful autobiographies of trans people.
- Is there a way you can contribute to healthy dialogue about gender issues between people with differing views?

Race

Womanist is to feminist as purple is to lavender.
Alice Walker (1983, pp. xi–xii)

At this stage in Goddess spirituality, we need to look at the effects of oppression and at the structures of power and privilege that facilitate and sustain oppression. The roots of intersectionality lie in black feminist thought and activism. Intersectionality applies to everyone and requires deep reflexivity and willingness to change, especially from the most privileged. Whiteness can be implicitly normative, even when diversity is explicitly expressed as a value and intention. An early illustration of intersectional activism is Sojourner Truth's famous speech in 1851, during which she asked "Ain't I a woman?" She placed black women's experiences and rights as central to the fight for women's rights.[16]

In the 1970s and 1980s, activists such as bell hooks, Angela Davis, Audre Lorde and the Combahee River Collective articulated the interdependence of sexist and racist systems, and the necessity of coalition politics to dismantle them. Recent books by black women that I consider well worth reading include *Hood Feminism* by Mikki Kendall (2021), *White Feminism* by Koa Beck (2021) and *Race, Gender, and Leadership* by Patricia Parker (2006).

In second-wave feminism, some women were race aware and actively encouraged attention to all facets of oppression, others less so. The perspective of womanism includes race and class-based oppression as integral to gender; 'womanist' was a term coined by Alice Walker (1983). The experiences of black women, black culture, black myths, oral tradition and spiritual life are the lenses through which their identity is shaped and experienced.

As I understand it, from my reading, a black woman's blackness is not a component of her feminism: her blackness is the lens through which she understands herself. I consider it vital that white people look at their own fragility, racism and white supremacy, as well as all their bias and prejudices. Only then can they be fully intersectional and use their white privilege skilfully.

The contribution of bell hooks, a black feminist writer, is phenomenal. I love her work. She examines the effect of racism and sexism on black women within feminist movements. She explains how the second-wave feminist movement was mostly white, middle and upper class, and did not articulate the needs of poor and black women. Women of colour and lesbians didn't get the same level of attention, and the number of black women who participated in the feminist movement in the 1970s was low. bell hooks has published more than 30 books; her most recent, *Feminism is for Everybody: Passionate Politics* (2000), is an invaluable overview of feminism. Her first major book, *Ain't I a Woman? Black Women and Feminism* (1981), was titled after Sojourner Truth's famous speech in 1851.

'Sacred Women of Africa and the African Diaspora: A Womanist Vision of Black Women's Bodies and the African Sacred Feminine' is a powerful article about womanism and the African sacred feminine (Razak, 2016).[17]

* * *

I welcome people of colour examining the whiteness and class of second-wave feminists. Mistakes and inappropriate responses were made and it's important that all anger and wounding can be expressed too. I welcome understanding, conciliation and restitution, without blame or diminishing of anyone, alongside genuine acknowledgement of the harm done.

Each wave and generation of feminism had its strengths and its weaknesses, and we can always do better. As a white person, I genuinely want to be part of the solution, not the problem, and to be an ally to people of colour as well as doing my own inner work and emotional labour. I continually explore my own white fragility and white supremacy, however painful that can be at times.

Perspectives and understandings shift and expand; I see that as a positive thing.

Reflection

1. What did you learn about your own race, culture and nationality when growing up?
2. What did you learn about people of other races, cultures and nationalities when growing up?

3. What differences did you become aware of?

4. How do you understand racism? What is prejudice? Is there a difference?

5. In what ways are you affected by racism? How has it shaped you?

6. Explore and understand the 'colour blind' approach to racism and the anti-racist approach.

7. How hard is it to accept any complicity with racism? If you can, how can you change?

8. What is white privilege?

9. How do you relate to the words 'white supremacy'?

10. What does whiteness mean to you?

Cultural Appropriation

Cultural appropriation involves borrowing from, or adopting attributes of, a culture not your own, for your own use. As an arena of exploration, it examines the history and actions of one culture towards another, and the balance of power between them.

Globalisation has made cultural cross-pollination inevitable. Cultural exchange is quite different, because exchange involves mutuality, consent and sharing. Cultural appreciation is respectful and affirmative. Incorporating other cultural influences into your work is fine, as long you openly and skilfully acknowledge where it originates from and give full credit. It can also involve financial compensation to those acknowledged and involved.

Cultural appropriation refers to a particular power dynamic in which members of a dominant culture take elements from the culture of people who have been systematically oppressed by that dominant group, or another one. Its usage was first adopted by indigenous peoples of nations tainted by histories of colonisation, such as Canada, Australia and the USA. All these countries have living, indigenous cultures that have been harmed and colonised. Appropriating can include unacknowledged or inappropriate adoption of customs, rituals, artefacts, practices, ideas, ceremonies, language, stories, songs, music, food, religious symbols, myths, clothing, deities and intellectual property, as well as belief systems. It is done by someone from a more dominant or oppressive culture, particularly colonial ones, taking from less economically and politically powerful groups. An example could be someone who claims to be a member of an indigenous tribe and the holder of their spiritual wisdom when it's not true. They refuse to give any acknowledgement or payment from their income to that tribe and make significant profit out of offering 'authentic indigenous wisdom'. If you claim a heritage and cultural identity not native to you, and which isn't acknowledged by the relevant indigenous tribe, lineage or community, you may be culturally appropriating.

I believe it is best to stay as close as possible to your own indigenous culture, especially in the UK, where the question of who is indigenous can be complex because of such widespread colonisation.

* * *

By coming to live in Glastonbury, I feel I have returned home to my ancestral roots and to Celtic Goddess spirituality. I consider myself part of the Brythonic or Brittonic heritage. The name 'Brythonic' was derived by Welsh Celticist John Rhys from the Welsh word 'Brython', meaning Ancient Britons rather than Anglo-Saxon or Gael.

Reflection

1. If you are inspired by an indigenous cultural heritage, what steps will you take to ensure that your work and actions evidence a respectful and responsible

collaboration?

2. Are you drawing on accurate knowledge and representations of that cultural heritage?

3. Are you disrespecting, in any way, the beliefs and values of those indigenous peoples?

4. Are you stereotyping?

5. How might you build a respectful relationship and collaboration with people from the indigenous cultural heritage you are inspired by?

6. How might you give clear acknowledgement and a financial contribution?

Chapter 3

Wisdom of the Goddess Luminary Leadership Wheel

Overview
Teaching and Learning Approach
Goddess Charge to Her Luminaries
Experiencing the Wheel
The Eight Dimensions of the Wheel

The Luminary Leadership training built on my traditional business leadership training and spiritual training; then took it to a whole new level. It went beyond patriarchal and dualist thinking, which still litters many current leadership programmes. [Lynne] draws on the interconnected and collaborative qualities required for 21st-century leadership. This is leadership training at Spiral Dynamic Second Tier, Yellow, or Flex-Flow. This training grows you both as a person and as a leader. I received insights into questions such as "If I am true to myself, how am I showing up and what should I be doing next as a leader?" The Paths of Power and dealing with toxic leaders were insightful, inspiring and empowering. Lynne embodies what she teaches, holding a strong and caring safe space. She is passionately devoted to empowering you to become the best version of yourself, as an individual and as a leader.
David, maieutic Luminary

Overview

We need a new myth, a new vision, a new definition of power and leadership. We must go away from the old model

and toward one of creative cooperation on our small and threatened planet. The world needs women to imagine, define and lead us toward a sane and sustainable culture. A culture of soul. A culture that values life more than war.
Johnnetta Cole (Feminist, n.d.)

How did the Wheel develop? I reflected on my own leadership journey and what had helped me most in all my leadership roles. I revisited, synthesised and integrated my leadership and spiritual experience and wisdom while walking the land. I sat in meditation to allow a new unfolding. I connected to the illumination of the moon and felt a flowing cyclical energy.

Initially the teachings came through me in poetic form as 'Goddess Charge to Her Luminaries'. Then the Goddess Luminary Wheel diagram emerged in the form of moons positioned in four moon phases and the four elemental directions, aligned to the Brigit-Anna Wheel. A cyclical Wheel felt appropriate to me for the non-linear way in which leadership manifests in real time, in any context. I chose blue as the primary colour as it is part of the moon colour spectrum. The four elements provide connection to nature and the earth. Goddess was in the centre. The eight different dimensions formed next, and all the words arose as non-gendered.

The word 'Luminary' resonated with me more than the usual word 'leader'. The originality of the Goddess Luminary Wheel lies in its unique synthesis of my extensive leadership, spiritual and teaching experience integrated with Goddess spirituality, moons and elements and holding ritual and ceremony. My own unique leadership development elixir.

Teaching and Learning Approach

As a qualified teacher and experienced leadership developer, I take a highly inclusive and learner-centred approach to learning. The Luminary journey facilitates your own unique developmental growth, rather than defining a particular end point or set of competences. I include a wide range of teaching and learning methods so that you can learn within your preferred learning style. I also encourage you to gain experience of other ways of learning, ones less comfortable or familiar, to stretch yourself. I include experiential, reflective, contemplative, conceptual, creative and embodied ways of learning. I provide information, guidance and sharing from my own knowledge, wisdom and experiences. I have designed strong holding processes so that each Cycle prepares you with skills and knowledge helpful for the other Cycles.

Each of the six Cycles has information on themes, a Luminary model, experiential exercises, an embodiment practice or ceremony, and plenty of reflection questions. Each Cycle has a resource section towards the end of the book. It has links to the chants, songs, videos and online literature to which I refer. For ease of access these are marked with number cues indicating their place in the Online Resources section.

I encourage you to draw upon and go deep into your own experiences, questions, understanding, issues and complexities. It is also important to persevere with parts of the Wheel that may create some resistance in you. Please go for it, expand your repertoire of ways of learning, push your boundaries and have a fabulous time.

* * *

The Wheel may look complex at first, but as I guide you through the eight dimensions all will become clear. I offer the analogy of learning to drive: it feels complex at first but with study, practice and experience all the interconnecting dimensions eventually fall into place. The Wheel is a hologram, which you can enter at any point to access its wisdom. It's cyclical rather than linear, designed to be adaptable and accessible from wherever your unique learning begins. You will be encouraged to go deeper into knowing yourself and diving into your preconceptions of what being a leader involves. You will be equipped to lead from your authenticity, unique voice, presence, healthy power and wisdom.

I have threaded quotes from students throughout the book to provide a flavour of how they have experienced the teachings and the impact it has had on them. In the face-to-face course, students are supported by me through feedback on regular assignments, one-to-one sessions and an action project.

Goddess Charge to Her Luminaries

Now I turn your attention to an important question. Is being a Goddess Luminary your call?

The Goddess Luminary Wheel, in poetic form, calls Her Luminaries to be luminous, loving and Leaderful, leading from Her power and love.

Let's approach the Charge through the reflection below.

Reflection

1. Is the Luminary journey the right one for you?
2. Reading a text as a sacred and deeply reflective act has been part of spiritual traditions for centuries and is an important spiritual practice for many modern people.
3. Read the text below as sacred words, meditatively and slowly, holding each word and phrase in your awareness and in your heart. Allow the Charge to affect you in every part of your being. Spiritual reading is different from our normal, analytical reading for information and entertainment. It involves a slow, meditative reading, reading not so much with the mind as with the heart.

* * *

4. Begin by reading the Charge below aloud or silently.
5. Read it slowly and meditatively two or three times, allowing the words to be absorbed and to affect you.

Goddess Charge to Her Luminary

She of ten thousand names and more
I am Goddess Gnosis,
Presence, Love, Birther,
Shining Illuminatrix.
Goddess of the four elements
Initiatrix of Air
Ignitrix of Fire
Connectrix of Water
Maturtrix of Earth
Goddess of archetypes
Seer, Activist, Healer, Guardian, Wisdom Keeper

Luminary
I am you and you are Me
I call you to be Leaderful
through direct knowing of Me
Through My Love and My Power.
Be My Presence wherever you lead
Birth the fullest potential of all.

Commune with Me always
Breathe Me in
Be the thinness of air
Reveal My feisty flames
Flow like holy water
Remain rooted in My land.
Be My radiance of Moon
New, Waxing, Full, Waning and Dark
Show the way, light the darkness.

Be Synchronous, Be in Service
In Flow and Emergence
Illuminate My Power from within.
Sense and Discern My will
Embody Me in action
Resonate My Divine energy
Serve through the wisdoms of
Head, Intuition, Heart and Body.
Be Aware, Autonomous
Adaptive and Authentic.

Travel through the underworld
Know the depth of dark moon
and your own shadow.
Cut through falseness and deceit.
Lead wisely in communities,
movements and organisations.
Beyond convention and patriarchy
Beyond domination and fear.
Lead by Power for, with and through
Birth magnificence in everyone.

Goddess Luminary .
Love, Listen and Liberate
Lead from fullness of lunar light
Lead from darkest brilliance of night
My luminous Presence in the world.

Blessed Be

6. Is there a word or phrase that jumps out at you? Allow
   yourself to become aware of any word or phrases that
   evoke a particular response. Do they speak deeply and
   positively, or perhaps produce resistance or reactivity in

you?

7. Now read the Charge again, lingering over this word or phrase. Pay attention to what resonates in you, to your own response to the words. Stay with the word or phrase and repeat or reread as often as feels right.

8. You may wish to spend 10–15 minutes meditating on the word or phrase by repeating it, aloud or silently, allowing the words to speak to you at an even deeper level.

9. What is Goddess teaching you? How is She guiding you through your response to this word or phrase?

10. Express your response through writing, drawing, prayer, dancing, singing or movement.

11. Do you feel called to live out any insight gained from your reading and experiencing of the Goddess Charge to Her Luminary?

May receiving Her Charge inspire you now to explore the Luminary Wheel in all its dimensions.

Experiencing the Wheel

Now, take some time to sit with the Goddess Luminary Leadership Wheel diagram (Figure 1).

Don't worry if it feels a little overwhelming; you don't have to understand or remember it all.

We will work through each dimension together.

Take your time; notice which parts of the Wheel you are drawn to.

What happens as you look at it?

Do particular words affect you? If so, note down which ones.

What is happening in your head, in your heart, your gut, and your body?

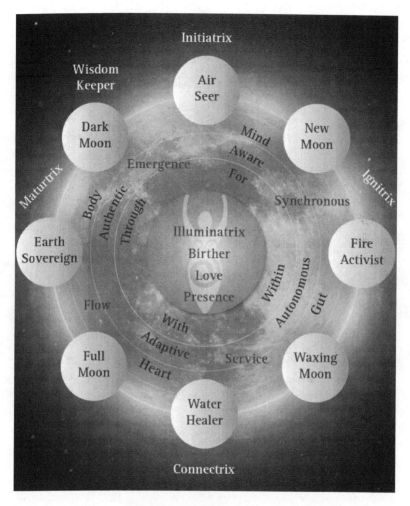

Figure 1 Goddess Luminary Leadership Wheel

The Eight Dimensions of the Wheel

There are eight dimensions on the Wheel, illustrated in linear form in the table below.

Each dimension has its own facets:

Goddess Gnosis	Natural Element	State of Being	Ways of Knowing
Birther	Air	Authentic	Head
Love	Fire	Aware	Intuition
Presence	Water	Autonomous	Heart
	Earth	Adaptive	Body
Archetype	**Moon Phase**	**Path of Power**	**Leaderful Way**
Illuminatrix	New	For	Synchronous
Initiatrix	Waxing	Within	Service
Ignitrix	Full	With	Flow
Connectrix	Dark	Through	Emergence
Maturtrix			
Wisdom Keeper			

Reflection

1. You may wish to return to the Wheel illustration and revisit how it now affects you.
2. Do you now see different patterns and connections?
3. Is the Wheel becoming clearer?

I now provide a brief overview of each dimension, which is explored in detail within the relevant Cycle.

Goddess Gnosis

The meaning of 'gnosis' is knowing, a direct and visceral knowing derived from direct experience, a direct, subjective, personal truth that feels deeply real. It may not fit into or be articulated through any concept that you know of with your mind. Goddess Gnosis is your personal unique truth of the direct experience and knowing of the Divine as Goddess, as sacred female. You will have space to explore and articulate your own Goddess Gnosis in depth as Goddess is at the centre of the Wheel, supporting you throughout. Some of you reading this will already have your own Goddess Gnosis; others may be new to exploring what Goddess means for you. Nurturing your own experience of Goddess is an exciting and fascinating journey.

Archetypes

There are six Luminary archetypes. At the centre of the Wheel is the archetype **Illuminatrix**. **Initiatrix** sits at the north and air. **Ignitrix** is at the west and fire. **Connectrix** sits at the south and water. **Maturtrix** is at the east and earth. **Wisdom Keeper** sits in the north-west and dark moon. Archetypes are valuable metaphors for self-understanding and coming to wholeness. They offer portals through which you can see your personality structures and gain new insights. The Luminary archetypes bring to life key facets of Goddess and Her elemental nature to assist your leadership journey. The beautiful images that introduce each Cycle were created specifically for my teachings by artist Kat Shaw.

Elements

The four natural elements of **air**, **fire**, **water** and **earth** provide direct connection and experience of the physical, energetic and elemental world. Ceremony focusing on each element and chanting is embedded in each Cycle. During your journey, you will walk the land, breathe in the air, dance around fire and bathe in or drink water to experience Goddess in elemental form.

Moon Phases

There are eight moon phases as the moon moves each month. Each moon cycle is 27 days long. I have included four moon phases: new, waxing, full and dark moon. You start your journey in **new moon** and move into your power and expansion with the growing illumination of **waxing moon**. At **dark moon** you go deep into your depths to reveal the brilliance of your shadow, and to let go and transform. At **full moon** you experience the magnificence and abundance of your Luminary Sovereignty.

State of Being

At the core of my Luminary teaching is the premise that the more expansive your way of being, the more you can be responsive, skilful and effective. The four states of being are authentic, aware, autonomous and adaptive. **Authentic**, the earth state, involves being true to who you really are and to your values. I have created a Goddess Luminary authenticity model which we will explore in Cycle I. **Aware**, the air state of being, enables you to understand how your internal reactions and responses are affecting you alongside the ability to know what you are doing, and why, as you do it. **Autonomous** is the fire state of being. This assists you in knowing and setting clear boundaries, being independent and able to make decisions from your own clarity and volition. It helps you to feel your own internal passion and feisty nature. **Adaptive** is the water state of being. You will explore this through the Luminary model of Interconnection. In this state you can be responsive and empathic, agile and in flow, with an open and emotionally wise heart.

Path of Power

It is important to understand your own personal relationship with power. Many of us have difficulty with the fullest expression of our own power. To help with this, I have created the Luminary Path of Power, which explores 17 different types and sources of power, conceptually and experientially. Becoming Luminary requires you to become clear about your personal relationship with your inner and outer power and how you manifest your own power, positively or negatively, genuinely understanding when you empower or disempower others.

Ways of Knowing

Goddess spirituality is an embodied path that encourages you to pay attention to your body. When you do that, you discover that you have a bodily intelligence and that each of your physical cells can sense and respond. The Wheel includes the practice of embodiment to explore how you lead from your body and stay grounded, resilient and physically healthy. I introduce wisdom from neuroscience to understand how your brain can help you to be more effective. Through the Luminary ways of knowing, you explore how head, intuition, heart and body all play a critical role in your wider intelligence and knowing system. You will move around the Wheel through these four different ways of knowing, learning how to access each one to become more aware and responsive.

The Leaderful Way

The Luminary Leaderful Way is the underpinning philosophy of the Wheel. I first came across the term 'Leaderful' in *The Empowerment Manual: A Guide for Collaborative Groups* (Starhawk, 2011), and then in the work of Joseph Raelin: *Creating Leaderful Organizations: How to Bring Out Leadership in Everyone* (2003) and *The Leaderful Field Book: Strategies and Activities for Developing Leadership in Everyone* (2010).

I have developed my own understanding of Leaderful, which includes synchronous, service, flow, emergence and Goddess Gnosis. These five Leaderful pathways are distinctive in themselves, yet when developed, integrated and practised simultaneously can bring liberation, high performance and fulfilment. Leaderful, for me, is an interconnected, plural, collective, collaborative and sharing endeavour rather than an individual phenomenon. Leadership no longer derives from charismatic or heroic influences but manifests as caring, loving people leading together interconnectedly and simultaneously, as peers, with a shared common purpose. A detailed exploration of the Luminary Leaderful Way can be found in my monograph.[18]

Goddess Gnosis is described above and in Cycle I. **Synchronous** means existing or occurring at the same time. It involves more than one leader stepping forward simultaneously, as well as encouraging others to co-lead. **Service** involves thinking and acting beyond yourself to make a wider contribution to serve the greater good and the larger picture. **Flow** is a state of effortless concentration and high absorption, becoming so completely involved and absorbed in an activity that nothing else seems to matter. Every action, movement and thought follows inevitably from the previous one. **Emergence** allows things to arise in organic and natural ways. It involves continually rethinking, aligning and adjusting to what is happening, considering new factors as they arise or are discerned. Emergent leaders encourage co-creation, innovation, constructive challenge, discernment and circle processes.

* * *

I hope this overview of the eight dimensions has whetted your appetite to learn more and to continue to Chapter 4 to journey through each Cycle of the Goddess Luminary Wheel.

Chapter 4

Journeying the Wheel

Overview
Cycle I Initiating Your Luminary Journey: Illuminatrix
Cycle II The Dance of Dreaming, Knowing and Awareness: Initiatrix
Cycle III Igniting Power, Passion and Intuition: Ignitrix
Cycle IV The Weave and Flow of Interconnection: Connectrix
Cycle V The Brilliance of Dark Moon: Wisdom Keeper
Cycle VI Maturing in Abundance and Sovereignty: Maturtrix

The Luminary Wheel programme has provided me with a steady support to develop the kind of boundaries I need to stay focused on my goals. This is a wonderful training course, and a safe space to grow; I highly recommend it. Attending and participating within the group has allowed me to recognise the gifts and values I share with the world. It also supported a strong sense of community, even in the midst of a global pandemic. Particularly special, in a time when Luminary hope and nurturing was so deeply needed.
Susannah, maieutic Luminary

Overview

It is good to have an end to journey towards, but it is the journey that matters, in the end.
Ursula K. Le Guin (1969, p. 219)

This chapter contains all the six Cycles. The overall structure for each Cycle includes:

- Title
- Luminary Archetype
- Dimensions
- Themes
- Introduction
- Being Present
- Calling In
- Checking In

Each Cycle begins with an introduction which provides an overview of the learning, content and themes of the Cycle. I suggest three ways you can prepare: being present, calling in and checking in. I encourage you to move gently, spiritually and purposefully into each Cycle. While it may feel repetitive, the purpose of repeating these three approaches every time is to encourage you to begin your learning by being present and deeply conscious of where you are, as you begin to explore the richness and content. I also encourage you to feel into your connection to Goddess and to be open to your own unique Goddess Gnosis and experience of Goddess.

Please take the time to do the opening spiritual practice. My experience is that this can make a huge difference to your concentration, to your energy and to your openness and expansiveness.

* * *

There is a Bibliography which references all the publications I mention. I have also included an Online Resources section for each chapter and Cycle with all the links in the relevant section. For the Cycles, this includes links to online publications, information, chants, songs and videos. The links are numbered so that you can find them easily.

* * *

Join me now on your individual developmental journey through the six Cycles and the eight dimensions of the Goddess Luminary Leadership Wheel. I hope you find your journey radical and edgy, yet also well grounded and practical.

Cycle I Initiating Your Luminary Journey

Illuminatrix

She who owns and expresses her Goddess-inspired Luminary shining brilliance, and illuminates others, enabling them to shine and to be their own magnificence.

Dimensions
Archetype: **Illuminatrix**
Direction: **Centre**
Path of Power: **Love**
State of Being: **Presence**
Leaderful Way: **Birther**
Ways of Knowing: **Goddess Gnosis**

Themes
Love Leadership, Birther, Goddess Gnosis, Why Would Anyone Be Led by You?, Leading with Presence, Maieutic Listening, Illumination Circles

Introduction

I feel Her as the natural energy in my body and of the world.
Starhawk (Christ and Plaskow, 1992, pp. 278–9)

At the centre of the Wheel is the archetype Illuminatrix: She who owns and expresses her Goddess-inspired Luminary shining brilliance, and illuminates others, enabling them to shine and to be their own magnificence.

This Cycle initiates you into your own unique Luminary journey by helping you to experience and deepen your Goddess Gnosis alongside understanding your identity as a leader. You explore how to lead from love and the creative power of Birther. You will directly experience and practise reflection and presence, learning how to become truly centred and grounded. I provide lots of different ways of learning, including contemplative, experiential, reflective, conceptual and practical.

In this Cycle you will:

- gain insight and confidence into your unique, authentic leadership journey
- know viscerally your Goddess Gnosis
- understand how love is important in leadership
- explore why anyone would be led by you
- learn about Illumination Circles
- experience a mix of learning styles
- begin practising presence to become fully centred and grounded
- explore the characteristics of successful activists.

Feel free (or not) to wear any shade of moon-blue colour clothes for any part of reading and exploring this Cycle.

Being Present

Before beginning, take time to get present in whatever way suits you best.

Centre yourself, by sitting, standing or walking, indoors or outdoors.

Notice your breathing, your posture and where your attention is. How deep can you go internally? How much is your attention drawn outwards? Go as deep and centred as you can.

Notice your thoughts; can you notice them without being drawn into them?

You may wish to sit still, sing or dance to the beautiful chant by Shawna Carol (2014), 'Be Still and Listen'.[19]

Calling In

In your own way, call in any Goddesses that you feel connected to. You may do this out loud or silently. Invoke whichever Goddess feels right for you. You may want to create an altar on which you place items of significance to you as you work through the themes and explorations of this first Cycle. Place items that say something you want to share about your relationship with Goddess, and however you connect and experience to the Divine, as directly as possible.

Checking In

Check in with where you are now, before you work through any part of this book; perhaps write in your journal or just notice and be aware of what is happening for you inside and out, here now. Stay as present as you can and notice what is happening to you. Find places on the land or indoors that feel safe, where you can relax, reflect and be exactly who you are. Write down how you are feeling, your thoughts, what is happening in your gut and body. What insights do you gain from your reflections?

Love Leadership

I deliberately open this first Cycle with love, a word many shy away from regarding leadership, but one that is important. My leadership is an offering of love into the world, my path of service and spiritual growth. It is also my way of fostering the potential and brilliance of others as well as fighting injustice and oppression. I love the world enough to stand up and speak my truth, to go against injustice and to be an ally to others.

I first used the word 'love' overtly in 1990, as a senior leader, when I was dean of Croydon Business School. Half the staff were appalled, and my deputies advised me to stop using it. I was only 35, new in post and surrounded by men, so I did stop; it felt too scary. By 1998, I had gained sufficient confidence, so when I was appointed as the new principal of Guildford College and we co-created a new college vision and values, it had the word 'love' in it. The staff transmuted love into the phrase 'love of learning', but it was there. I was ahead of my time and am delighted to say that in the 2020s it is not uncommon to hear the word 'love' openly mentioned in relation to leadership.

The first book I read on love was James Autry's *Love and Profit: The Art of Caring Leadership* (1991). He probably felt compelled to link it directly with profit to be acceptable, but it was still a breakthrough book.

I then discovered the competing management approaches of Theory X and Theory Y. Theory X proposes that managers work through fear, and that everyone is lazy unless you push and control them. Theory Y, on the other hand, emphasises having high trust and believing that everyone is genuinely doing their best. This can be translated into the spiritual lens of do you lead from fear or from love? I am an extreme Theory Y person and do my best to lead from love. Not a fluffy kind of love, as I know that deep, authentic love can be tough and fierce and challenging as well as kind, embracing, expansive and empowering.

A more recent book you might enjoy is *Love to Lead* (Kite, 2018), which offers practical ways of leading and loving, especially in coaching. Often the issue of vulnerability arises when we try to be open and expansive, so I really recommend *Dare to Lead: Brave Work, Tough Conversations, Whole Hearts* by Brené Brown (2018), who writes so powerfully on vulnerability and shame. You may also be interested in her online Dare to Lead Hub.[20]

A more general book on love is *All About Love: New Visions* (hooks, 2001), a powerful exploration of how to love in a society that doesn't encourage the levels of connection and intimacy she knows are possible.

I experience Goddess as love, She who creates, holds and nurtures all living beings and all forms of nature. I have no desire to dominate, only to love, foster and nourish everyone, and every form, to its fullest potential. Like everyone else, I express my own unique flavour of Goddess through my personal essence and actions in the world. From my spiritual experiences, I can only love and honour the earth and every life form on our planet.

Two ways I have expressed love in my professional life is through my commitment to diversity and inclusion, and by proactively encouraging staff to bring their whole selves into the workplace.

In all the organisations I led, the core value of diversity, and permission to be your fullest unique self, was fostered by co-creating a culture in which differences were truly celebrated and respected within a meaningful and common purpose. At the Centre for Excellence in Leadership, to understand diversity, we did appreciation exercises and activities that enabled us to 'walk in one another's shoes' on away days. As the offices were based in London – a multicultural, highly diverse city – we attracted people of many different faiths and of no faith. For those who had trouble bringing their spirituality or other parts of themselves into the workplace, we created Dignity at Work days. Profound discussions emerged among the highly diverse staff from more than 10 countries, who between them spoke 15 different languages and were from a wide range of ethnicities. Diversity awareness training was available for all staff and included space to explore all facets of diversity. They learned that disrespecting other faiths, beliefs, cultures and individuals, in any way, was not acceptable in the organisation. The diversity discourse was held in a respectful and loving manner to enable people, with the support of trained facilitators, to work though their own prejudices and biases.

I want you to think deeply about your relationship to love and how that helps you to reframe or understand how you want to be a leader in the world. The Luminary Wheel has love at its centre and unashamedly explores and lives love, in all its shapes and expressions.

Reflection

1. How can you lead from love? What would it involve?
2. What is your relationship to love and fear?
3. How vulnerable can you be with others?

Birther

For me, Goddess is the Birther from which both women and men are derived; Her matrix creates and holds and nurtures all living beings. She loves everyone and everything she births, therefore cannot include the oppression or diminishing of anyone or anything. She dissolves all separation and the oppression or diminishing of anyone or anything.

I have written a Goddess creation story, below, for you to read in the way you did for the Luminary Charge, as sacred words, meditatively and slowly, allowing it to affect you in every part of your being.

Goddess Creation Myth

Goddess dances beyond time,
beyond beginnings and endings
She always has, and always will
Birthing the fabric of reality
Weaving Her delicate web
Of unbroken connection
Her resilient warp and weft supporting, uniting
expanding and creating
Goddess sings as well as dances
sounding the word LOVE
A powerful resonating cacophony
Calling forth new creations
Breathing life into form
Skies, stars and planets coalesce from Her trailing swirls of air
The oceans stream from Her tears of joy
Fire ignites from Her passion
She shines the moon and lights the sun
Earth arises from the fecundity of Her womb
Fertilised by depth of LOVE
Embodied in elements of
Air, Fire, Water and Earth
From Her womb, the abundant manifestation of Human creation
Their form released to love and procreate here on earth
And Earth flourishes
Its beauty and fecundity flowing
Everything living in harmony
Plants, animals, birds, insects, mammals, grain
All that is and can become
Nourishing and flourishing
Constantly creating and transforming through the cycles

Of birth, living, decay, death and rebirth
Each a part of the cyclical web and flow
Flowering in grace, eldering into wisdom
Holding both shadow and light
Returning to the Earth to be reborn
Goddess sings to all in the whispering of the wind
Warms through the heat of fire
Purifies in the cleansing flow of water
Nourishes with Her earthly abundance
Hoping none will forget the Mother of us all
Dance with Goddess
Weaving together in LOVE
In Her delicate web of unbroken connection
Feeling Her resilient warp and weft
Supporting and uniting
Constantly expanding and creating

Blessed Be

1. Begin by reading the story aloud or silently.
2. Read it slowly and meditatively two or three times, allowing the words to affect you.
3. Is there a word or phrase that jumps out at you? Allow yourself to become aware of any word or phrase that evokes a particular response.
4. Now read the story again, lingering over this word or phrase. Pay attention to what resonates in you, to your own response to the words. Stay with the word or phrase and repeat or reread as often as feels right.
5. You may wish to spend 10–15 minutes meditating on the word or phrase by repeating it, aloud or silently, allowing the words to speak to you at a deep level.
6. What is Goddess teaching you? How is She guiding you through your response to this word or phrase?

7. Do you want to express this through writing, drawing, prayer, dancing, singing or movement?

Goddess Gnosis

I perceive a web of relatedness and love within the world and I choose to put a feminine form to that energy – to name it and know it as Goddess.

Molly Remer (Feminism and Religion, 2012)

Some of you reading this will already have your own direct experience of Goddess. Others may be new to exploring what Goddess means for you. Nurturing your own experience of Goddess can be an exciting and fascinating journey. The meaning of 'Gnosis' is knowing, a direct and visceral knowing derived from direct experience; it is a direct, subjective, personal truth that feels deeply real. It may not fit into or be articulated through or contained within any concept that you may know of with your rational mind. Goddess Gnosis is *your* personal, unique truth, experience and knowing of the Divine as sacred female expression and quality. Some people refer to this direct knowing, beyond the usual understanding of rational mind, as mystical knowing or realisation. Each person's Goddess Gnosis is unique. For many people, Goddess is physically, spiritually, energetically and personally interconnected. She is everywhere within the web and matrix of all life. Goddess can be experienced as a verb rather than a noun; something to *BE*. She can also be experienced as a metaphysical presence.

Goddess spirituality sees sacredness in all of nature rather than seeing nature as something to be dominated, exploited or controlled. It celebrates the bounty and beauty of female bodies as well as nature's abundance. There is a direct relationship with the cyclical and natural elements of air, fire, water and earth, as well as the land, animals, moon and sun. Goddess spirituality fosters an earth-based sacred relationship to Gaia. Darkness and light are included, as well as depth and height. Birth and death are viewed as renewal and transformation. The female body is imbued with sacredness.

The honouring of Goddess is expressed through ceremony and ritual using female symbols, myths, images, invocations, songs, blessings and sacred drama. All these are designed to actively encourage creative ways of knowing and expression through art, poetry, music, intuition and the valuing of women's bodies, including womb power and the capacity to give birth.

My Goddess Gnosis experiences Her in the land: She is Gaia and Mother Earth. My female body is Her embodiment and I feel Her creative powers through the Earth, and the whole universe. I am Her and She is me. She is nature and we are an expression and embodiment of Her. There is no duality, no separation of any kind: Earth, Gaia, nature is the body of Goddess. She is equally present in places far away and close to home. We can find Her in our own local landscape.

I am a panentheist, so I experience Goddess as within, immanent, and bigger than me. I have a loving and beautiful relationship with her simultaneously as personal deity, as interconnected oneness and as a web of powerful, benign energy holding innumerable qualities, including light, love, beauty, decay, darkness and death. For me, Goddess is physically, spiritually, energetically and personally everywhere, the flow, web and matrix of all life. A pantheistic perspective views Goddess purely as immanence.

Reflection

1. How do you experience your Goddess Gnosis?
2. How do you relate, or not, to Goddess, to the Divine being female?
3. Can you articulate your own Goddess Gnosis through words, sound or visual images?
4. How do you feel in Her presence?
5. How does the Luminary Wheel help you to relate to your leadership?
6. How might Goddess-centred leadership be part of your life?
7. Do you have a view about the place of Goddess in your leadership?
8. How do, or might you, foster Goddess spirituality through your leadership?

Exercise

1. Get comfortable and relax. Find and listen to 'I Am the Goddess', a chant by Lisa Thiel.[21]
2. How do the words affect you? Notice what is happening. Journal if you want to.

* * *

3. Now explore visual images of Goddess and how they affect you. Find and watch these two videos: *You Gotta*

Believe by Nina Paley[22] and *The Heart of the Goddess* by Hallie Austen.[23]

4. Draw, sculpt, dance or write your creative expression of Goddess. Whatever arises here now.

* * *

5. Explore books on Goddess by inspiring writers such as Kathy Jones, Starhawk, Carol P. Christ, Lucy Pearce, Mary Daly and Merlin Stone. Find other writers. Hallie Austen also has a beautiful book: *The Heart of the Goddess: Art, Myth and Meditations of the World's Sacred Feminine* (2018).

6. Discuss Goddess spirituality with others to gain different perspectives.

7. Articulate for yourself what Goddess means, or can mean, for you in your life and work.

Embodiment Practice

1. Spend time sitting, walking and being present to the ways in which you experience Goddess through the land. Leave your phone at home. Listen to the sounds, feel the air, notice your breath and see the beauty all around you. Walk with your bare feet on whatever surface you can, especially grass or sand. Notice when you are grounded or not.

2. How does doing this affect you?

3. What happens to your energy when you walk the land?

4. What in nature makes you expansive?

5. How do you experience Goddess in the land?

6. How are you connected to others, to nature and to the planet?

Why Would Anyone Be Led by You?

I first found this phrase in a book of the same name, *Why Should Anyone Be Led by You? What It Takes to Be an Authentic Leader* (Goffee and Jones, 2006), which I taught for several years on leadership courses. I designed the repeating question exercise below, with the word 'would' rather than 'should', and discovered that it worked well with hundreds of people. I practise repeating questions as one of my spiritual practices, as a Diamond Heart student, and discover something significant every time.

A repeating question exercise literally means that one person keeps asking another person the same question in a present and skilful way. The other person answers with whatever arises.

I suggest you find someone you trust and do this exercise together. One person asks the question for 10 or 15 minutes; then swap over. Try and keep answers short; the purpose is to be spontaneous and allow whatever comes to mind to be spoken, without editing or long pauses, but don't rush.

Exercise

1. Take 10 minutes each to ask and answer, in turn, the question "Why would anyone be led by you?"
2. Then both individually reflect on your experience.
3. Next identify three reasons why someone would be led by you.
4. Share and discuss your reasons and your experience.
5. Reflect on and journal whatever has arisen for you.

Leading with Presence

Lynne taught me how to cultivate presence, what it feels like to be seen and heard when you are coming from that place of gnosis, of Divine presence. I remember her saying right at the beginning of the Luminary course about the conscious balance of a leader's outer and inner awareness in the room. I now understand when my awareness extends outwards or is directed inwards, and by how much. I was always scattered and too buffeted by others' energy. I now understand that in that centred, grounded, deeply coherent state we are fully available to respond. Hearing, in a new clustered thinking way that allows for multiple new connections to arise, offering non-polarising solutions of both/and, rather than either/ or. This has enabled me to offer workshops for women in UEA with a whole new level of depth, presence and impact.

Julie Trope, maieutic Luminary

From 1990, I began intense explorations into the notion of presence, in my personal spiritual practice, and experimenting with being present in my daily organisational life. It has taken me more than 20 years to understand how to consciously manifest presence, through an iterative process of experimentation and deliberate cultivation. Presence fascinates me and has played a major role in my life. Practising presence has deeply influenced my leadership in my workplaces and has remained a central and vital aspect of my spiritual inquiry and growth.

Being in the now, being present or experiencing presence, has become an important concept, experience and practice for some people; yet for many it is a mystery. It may feel unattainable, and beyond reach, even though it interests them. Most religious and spiritual traditions include presence. There has been a resurgence of interest in modern times, beyond the field of religion and spirituality into other disciplines. Presence is a key concept within philosophical traditions, the acting and healing professions and, more recently, is significant within modern leadership and organisational development.

Presence can be a spiritual experience or an experience of being in the moment without any spiritual connotation. Whatever the perspective, for most people, presence has a palpable quality of 'thereness' or 'isness' experienced as very real. Presence experiences may differ, but usually involve a natural stillness or feeling of deep peace. It may involve an inner knowing that "all is well", or a feeling of pure contentment, in which needs and attachments fall away.

For me, spiritually it means going beyond myself into an expansive, non-doing and receptive state. In the realm of being present and interacting with others, it includes awareness of what is happening in my physical body. I also become aware of own internal reactivity and personality needs and how my emotions are being stimulated. I feel fully immersed in what is happening, here now, without ego filters, and I can feel into what is most appropriate and skilful in the context I am in. I find the ability to be responsive to whatever arises, as well as seeing and manifesting new possibilities.

Effective leaders take time each day to deepen their daily spiritual practice and eventually to cultivate the capacity to be present constantly.

The **Luminary Presence model** (Figure 2) is a synthesis of the four Luminary states of being: aware, autonomous, adaptive and authentic. Its purpose is to support you in being more conscious in developing and practising presence. I suggest it as a core practice for every Luminary.

Luminary Presence is being fully in the moment, here now through directly experiencing Goddess Gnosis and being able to respond appropriately to whatever happens, however challenging, easy or unexpected. It draws on all or each of the Luminary states of being, as appropriate.

Aware is being conscious of how your internal responses are affecting you, and others, alongside the ability to know what you are doing as you do it, as well as understanding why you are doing it.

Autonomous is about having boundaries, alongside a healthy

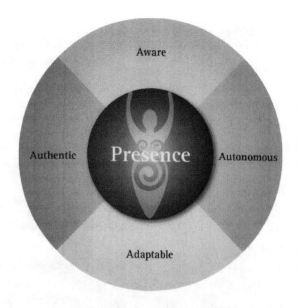

Figure 2 Luminary Presence

balance of independence and connection. An autonomous person can support and foster the independence of others. You consciously use your power to liberate. You can manage your own reactivity and behave skilfully.

Adaptable is being responsive and having empathy, high emotional intelligence and awareness of your impact on others. You have internal agility and can be in flow.

Authentic involves knowing, articulating and living your true self, steeped in Goddess and expressing all Her qualities. You will explore this more deeply in the next Cycle.

Maieutic Listening

Maieutic listening has a deeply spiritual character, as well as being very practical and valuable. It is an intentional attunement to the fundamental tone of the innermost being of ourselves and others. Its purpose is to help birth, in another, new insights and discernment, thus helping another to access and bring forth their own deep wisdom, discernment, creativity and illumination, without intervening with your own advice or perspective.

The maieutic stance is based on the understanding that true inner responsiveness depends on our capacity not to react immediately when someone has finished speaking, but to give ourselves time to heed fully what has been said; perhaps, to give it a second, more inward hearing. The practice of maieutic listening prepares the ground for a special type of intuitive perception or insight. Maieutic listening is the cultivation of an intimacy achieved through inner listening contact with others. It has the character of a direct and unmediated relationship of two people relating to their own, and each other's, inner being. Not only hearing what is being said but also noticing what's not being said through tone, body language, eye gaze and energy. The origin of the word 'maieutic' is the Greek *maieutikos*, relating to midwifery, from *maia*, 'midwife'.

Illumination Circles

Illumination circles are a key tool of the Luminary. I designed and adapted my process from Quaker clearness committees and their application by Margaret Benefiel. I was impressed with their impact on students when we used it in her Soul of Leadership programme. It may not feel appropriate now, as you read the book, as it is a group process. It may be worth looking at eventually. I use it a key support and exploration process throughout the course, and for students to stay connected between sessions, so I want you to be aware of it, hence its inclusion.

The purpose of illumination circles is for each member, when it is their turn, to be the inquiry person, and to receive support, insight and illumination on a key issue they bring to the circle. Other circle members speak and respond from deep discernment and wisdom. They do this through silence, maieutic listening, responsive questioning and by offering skilful and relevant comments.

Collectively everyone holds a sacred, safe container in which everyone can share and learn.

These all help the inquiry person to access and bring forth their own deep wisdom, discernment, creativity and illumination through receiving support, insight and illumination themselves.

Guidelines for Circle Members

1. Feel into what most helps the inquiry person, not you.
2. Trust your deepest intuition and wisdom to arise.
3. Notice where you are speaking from: presence, head, heart, gut, calm, reactivity or compassion.
4. Be aware of the tone of your voice and any charge that it may hold.
5. Be aware of the impact of your words on the inquiry person.
6. Do not give advice or tell the inquiry person what to do.
7. Offer thoughtful, relevant suggestions or questions, not advice; really try to discern the difference.
8. Do not speak across others; speak one at a time.
9. Don't try and fill the silence; only speak what is deep and authentic.

Process

Sit together in a circle. First, someone decides to bring something of significance for them into the circle and thinks of a leadership issue to work on; they become the inquiry person. You will each have a turn. One of you is the timekeeper, and one is the note-taker who writes down the questions and comments for the inquiry person to take away. Everyone stays present and attentive throughout.

Each circle takes approximately 40 minutes, or longer if you collectively decide this.

1. Settle into silence, holding the inquiry person in your attention (2 minutes).

2. The inquiry person speaks: everyone else is deeply present and offers open, attentive, respectful, loving maieutic listening, in silence, without interrupting the inquiry person at all. You listen not only to the words spoken, but also to feelings, nuances, body language and tone (7 minutes).

3. Next, move into informational and clarifying questions from each circle member, such as "How many people are involved?" or "What is the timescale?" (3 minutes).

4. Take another two minutes of collective silence, holding the inquiry person and the decision or situation with your three brains: that is, rationally, intuitively and compassionately (2 minutes).

5. In this stage, the inquiry person doesn't speak or respond to what is offered at all. Circle members, in presence, openness of heart, spirit and mind, with your full attention, love and respect, begin to ask questions and make helpful comments, without giving any form of advice. The note-taker writes down the questions and comments for the inquiry person to take away. Remember, the purpose of the questions and comments is to help illuminate the inquiry person, enabling them to go deeper, to reflect, to see a broader perspective, to birth new insights, to access and bring forth their own deep wisdom, discernment, creativity and illumination (15 minutes).

6. The inquiry person responds with any insight or illumination they have received (5 minutes).

7. The inquiry person shares their experience of this circle process (5 minutes).

8. The inquiry person chooses to end their circle turn

with silence, a song, a blessing, a healing, or whatever they would like to receive at this time. Circle members respond (2 minutes).

9. The circle closes with everyone bowing or hugging, in respect and gratitude.

10. You may wish to explore and share anything that arose together (own time allocation).

Closing Chant

1. Play Shawna Carol's chant, 'Be Still and Listen'.[24]

2. Really centre yourself in being still and being Goddess, knowing Her presence.

3. What arises for you now?

4. How does it feel?

5. How are you impacted?

Closing Reflection

Now take time to reflect on all you have learned and experienced in this Cycle. Let it integrate within you. Revisit anything you feel isn't yet complete. When you feel ready, in your own time, move into the next Cycle.

Cycle II The Dance of Dreaming, Knowing and Awareness

Initiatrix

She who swirls and unfolds, breathing the boundless, unlimited and free. Flying through all obstacles. Seer of visions, inspiring our dreaming and creativity.

Dimensions
Archetype: **Initiatrix**
Direction: **North**
Element: **Air**
Moon: **New**
Path of Power: **For**
State of Being: **Aware**
Leaderful Way: **Synchronous**
Way of Knowing: **Overview** and **Head**

Themes
Being Authentic, SelfAwareness Approaches, Ways of Knowing, Synchronous, Clearing Conversations

Introduction

Leadership is turning precious energy into matter: the energy of ideas and purpose into things that matter in people's lives. **Ginny Whitelaw** (Integral Life, n.d.)

At the north of the Wheel is air and the archetype Initiatrix: She who swirls and unfolds, breathing the boundless, unlimited and free. Flying through all obstacles. Seer of visions, inspiring our dreaming and creativity.

In this Cycle, you become conscious of how to lead, support, behave, and to co-create the best outcome for all involved. You will understand different ways of knowing and not knowing. You explore authenticity and self-awareness, two approaches used extensively in leadership development and on spiritual paths, and learn the importance of safety in fostering the thriving and potential of others. It includes the contribution of neuroscience, a new area of study that is revolutionising leadership. You explore the Luminary Authenticity model and experiment with flying in murmuration flocks; you directly experience the element of air, feeling Her presence in every breath. Goddesses of Air and Initiatrix inspire your learning, understanding and insights.

It is the place on the Luminary Wheel of visioning, initiating and being synchronous with others.

In this Cycle you will:

- explore and express your authenticity
- experience the clarity and alignment of drawing consciously on your three brains

- explore the potential to be in Leaderful synchronicity with others
- learn the qualities of enabling others to thrive and feel safe
- understand the difference between knowing, unknowing and allowing
- practise clearing conversations.

Feel free (or not) to wear grey, silver and pale blue colour clothes for any part of reading and exploring this Cycle.

Being Present

Before beginning, take time to get present in whatever way suits you best.

Centre yourself, by sitting, standing or walking, indoors or outdoors.

Notice your breathing, your posture and where your attention is. How deep can you go internally? How much is your attention drawn outwards? Go as deep and centred as you can.

Notice your thoughts; can you notice them without being drawn into them?

Take time to really notice what is happening in your mind as you get present. Are thoughts running through constantly? How can you relax your head here now?

Turn your attention to your breath; if it helps to keep your attention, count your breaths.

Connect with the element of air. Go outside and breathe in the air; notice your breath. How does breathing in more deeply affect your body? Your energy? Is your mind feeling more alert and clearer?

You may wish to dance gracefully, swirling in the air.

* * *

I share a poem I have written:

Breath of Life
With your breath You fill my body
I feel You dancing through my flesh
Gifting me vitality
Everything new and fresh

Breathing in the Goddess
Breathing in Her love
Breathing in Her sacred air
Below, around, above

With Your breath You fill the ethers
I fly Your soaring clouds and mist
Gifting me vitality
By You my soul is kissed

Calling In

In your own way, call in the element of air or one or more air Goddesses: whatever feels 'right' for you. You may want to create an altar on which you place items of significance as you work through the themes and explorations. Place items that say something you want to share about your relationship with your mind and your authenticity, or that help connect you to the element of air, or a specific air Goddess.

Checking In

Check in with where you are now, before you work through any part of this Cycle; perhaps write in your journal or just notice and be aware of what is happening for you inside and out, here now.

Being Authentic

The Luminary programme revealed a Leaderful, authentic part of me, which is committed to helping others connect to their authentic soul's radiant essence and to heal what is ready to heal. I now have new skills to bring to my teaching and have created two brand new training courses. I feel I am able to be a present teacher, enjoying and allowing the emergence of whatever wants to occur whilst holding the circle of students. Through Lynne's teaching of the Enneagram, I have learned that not everyone thinks, acts or wants the same as me! This ancient system has been invaluable in helping me understand why people do, behave and react the way they do. It really helps take the personal out of things, which is so important in holding circles and teaching.

Rachel, Goddess Luminary

One of the four Luminary states of being is authentic. Authentic leadership is an approach to leadership that emphasises building the leader's legitimacy through honest relationships built on integrity, self-awareness, accurate self-knowledge and openness. An authentic leader reflects upon all their actions and decisions and examines their own strengths and weaknesses. They are truthful and open in their interactions with others, leading from their head, intuition and heart. Authentic leaders are not afraid to name the reality of any situation, and willingly share their true selves with others. How they positively lead at work mirrors how they lead their private lives. They speak from their heart with passion, have a committed point of view, and are open and willingly articulate their ideas without any game-playing or hidden agendas.

Books I really like include *Who Do We Choose to Be? Facing Reality, Claiming Leadership, Restoring Sanity* (Wheatley, 2017); *On the Path to Authentic Leadership: The OPAL Way to Leadership Success* (Bown, 2017a) and *Why Should Anyone Be Led by You?*

What It Takes to Be an Authentic Leader (Goffee and Jones, 2006).

I have developed a Luminary model of authentic self (Figure 3), with the five facets of self-awareness, self-esteem, self-knowing, self-acceptance and self-agility, to help you to understand what is involved, and how to be more authentic in your own life and leadership. As you can see, it has Goddess Gnosis at the centre to remind us to stay grounded and present to Goddess.

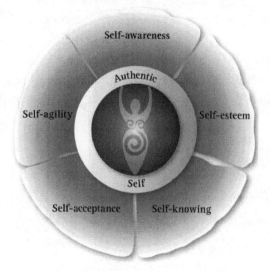

Figure 3 Luminary Authenticity

Authentic Self

Authenticity is one of the Luminary states of being and involves alignment between what you say and what you do, being true to yourself and your personal values. It is supported and fostered through presence. An authentic person puts the people around them at ease through being genuine, because this enables others to be genuine too. Authenticity fosters strength of character, especially when others are pressuring you to act in a way that you know is wrong, or in challenging situations. When a leader's integrity and authenticity is recognised by others, and feels predictable, it builds trust. A Luminary integrates, knows, articulates and lives their authentic self, aware of who they are and their balance of personality and connection to Goddess.

Self-Awareness

Cultivating self-awareness is so important. It involves being aware of how your internal responses and any reactivity are affecting you and others. It also involves the ability to witness *what* you are doing, *as* you do it, while simultaneously understanding *why* you are doing it. It requires the motivation to understand your inner life and your impact on others. You also need to identify the concepts you have and the stories you tell yourself, as well as your personality patterns and your shadow. This includes both your positive and wounded aspects. As a leader, the more practised you are at reading yourself, the more effective you will be. When a leader is self-aware, it gives others a feeling of safety, even in uncertain environments. A self-aware, leader modulates their behaviour to alleviate any stress and works to create an environment in which motivation and creativity flourish.

Self-Esteem

Self-esteem refers to a person's internal sense of their value or worth, and how much they intrinsically approve of or like themselves, or not. It also relates to the level of confidence you have in your own ability and contribution, and how much you appreciate and like yourself, regardless of the circumstances or what others may say or think about you. Self-esteem is what we think, feel and believe about ourselves, while self-worth is more related to an internal and external recognition that we are valuable human beings, worthy of love. Self-confidence is based more on external measures of success and value than the internal measures that contribute to self-esteem. One can have high self-confidence, particularly in a certain area or field, but still lack a healthy sense of overall value or self-esteem.

Self-Knowing

This involves understanding your personal values, beliefs and personality, knowing about your tendencies, thoughts, preferences and habits, skills and areas of weakness or limitation.

It takes deep work to see your concepts, personality patterns and shadow, both positive and negative. Authentic leaders go much deeper than their life story, what they have been through, or the issues they have. They embrace their true self and their ethical values, along with their weaknesses, and use their strengths without worrying about what others think. Self-knowing is the perception that we have of ourselves, our answer when we ask ourselves the question "Who am I?"

Self-Acceptance

When we can accept ourselves, we feel comfortable with who we are and can be kind and loving to ourselves. Truly authentic leaders accept and love themselves. Self-acceptance can lead to self-compassion and taking better care of our health and wellbeing, as well as stopping being harsh or overly critical of ourselves. When you accept yourself, you don't feel deficient as you can recognise that you have both strengths and weaknesses, without guilt or self-blame. You know who you are, and that feels fine. Self-acceptance liberates, with a sense of freedom to be more fully who you were meant to be, in your own unique way, with your talents and challenges. This can also include knowing when you don't know something, accepting this and acting appropriately without shame or embarrassment.

Self-Agility

This involves an internal state of being agile, being able to move, shift perspective and respond skilfully to others. To be agile involves learning to manage your own reactivity. You have to become more conscious of what drives your behaviour. It is linked to the other facets of authenticity, and the more experienced you are in all of them, the more agile you can be. Self-agility helps you to increase your sensitivity to your own internal emotions and instincts, parts we rarely access with our conscious mind. It also helps with your understanding and awareness of how you impact on others. It enables you to behave skilfully and to enhance and improve your relationships.

Reflection

1. In which facets are you strong?
2. Which do you need to develop?
3. Take one strong facet and celebrate how well you do this by writing in your journal, drawing, painting, making a sculpture or creating a poem or a song.
4. Take one facet you need to develop and reflect on what you will do to change or improve it.

Embodiment Practice

Find a sound bath if you can. We experience one together on the course; it can be so relaxing for your mind.

Self-Awareness Approaches

Since 1978, when I started work in education, I have experimented consistently with being a self-aware, reflective practitioner. Initially, I developed my reflective skills through working in action learning sets. As a lecturer, I explored how self-reflection and self-awareness facilitated my professional competence and my interpersonal relationships.

In 1989, as a leader, I discovered William Torbert's action inquiry in *The Power of Balance: Transforming Self, Society and Scientific Inquiry* (1991) and *Action Inquiry: The Secret of Timely and Transformational Leadership* (2004). He came to my business school and helped me integrate reflection into organisational life, as well as into my daily spiritual practice.

The work of Almaas, especially *The Inner Journey Home: The Soul's Realization of the Unity of Reality* (2004), has taught me how to live in continual inquiry as a way of life. More latterly, the more embodied spiritual practices of the Avalonian priestess tradition have grounded me into another dimension of deep presence through the land. In my experience, self-awareness is helped not only by looking at it from a spiritual and development perspective, but also through understanding and strengthening our conscious connection to all three of our brain regions.

Deep self-awareness takes practice and commitment, and most people choose a particular self-awareness approach to help them on their journey. Options include 360-degree feedback processes, coaching, the Enneagram, neurolinguistic programming (NLP), Myers-Briggs, the Big Five and Simon Western's 'Western indicator of leadership discourses' (Wild) questionnaire.

I encourage you to find an approach that really helps you and supports your insights.

My preferred self-awareness approach is the Enneagram, which I have been using for myself, my family and friends, and in work situations, since 1994. I have trained with many of the most respected Enneagram teachers in the world, including Don Riso, Russ Hudson, Helen Palmer, David Daniels, Sandra Maitri, Almaas and Ginger Lapid-Bogda, as well as in the Ridhwan spiritual school. The Enneagram has enthralled and fascinated me for over 30 years, and I am still learning so much about myself and others because of it. If you want to learn about the Enneagram, the best introduction is *The Wisdom of the Enneagram: The Complete Guide to Psychological and Spiritual Growth for the Nine Personality Types* (Riso and Hudson, 1999).

I have worked with the Enneagram as a chief executive in three different organisations in further education, as an Enneagram consultant for several charities and with boards of private companies. I also teach workshops. I must have used it with nearly 500 people. In the face-to-face Goddess Luminary Wheel training, students have found it to be an invaluable complement to their leadership and personal development. I am an Enneagram type Eight, with a Seven Wing, social. Throughout my career, I have engaged with self-awareness and profiling tests, and scored highly on all of them.

Reflection

1. How have you developed your own self-awareness?
2. Which approach has worked best for you?
3. If you haven't used a self-awareness approach, explore the possibilities and find one you like.

Ways of Knowing

An understanding of different ways of knowing is important, because leadership involves decision-making and constantly needing to understand and make sense of things, people and situations. One of the barriers good leaders need to move through is having a need to know everything. Heroic leadership perspectives pushed leaders into being the one everyone turns to. The Luminary Leaderful way encourages being open to listening and being adept at knowing the best questions to ask rather than having all the answers.

Two recent, important and exciting strands happening in leadership development involve the inclusion of multiple intelligences and the findings of neuroscience to assist leaders to be more effective. Both strands encourage a crossover between science and spirituality, between rational and intuitive ways of knowing. Many of us in leadership positions, who also have spiritual lives and sensibilities, have known and experienced the value of this crossover for years. The Luminary Wheel gives attention to all parts of ourselves and integrates the rational, emotional, spiritual and the practical.

Multiple Intelligences

Multiple intelligences have been around for a while, and different people choose different ones. This is my own personal list of intelligences from experience and study: nature, sound, spatial, aesthetic, reasoning, practical, experiential, interpersonal, kinaesthetic, verbal, ethical, emotional and spiritual. We each have natural ability in some and may find others quite hard. I have no spatial knowing: I cannot tell my left from my right, and can get lost going round the corner, literally. I cannot read maps at all. I have tried numerous times to improve my spatial way of knowing but have failed to date.

In their seminal research work, *Women's Ways of Knowing: The Development of Self, Voice, and Mind*, Belenky et al (1986) found that a woman does not think or reason like a man, nor does she look at those in authority the same way. This is due to her experiences and interactions with parents, culture and her economic situation. They identified five stages of a woman's development: silence, received, subjective, procedural and constructed knowledge. This work has been used widely in supporting the development of many women. I read the research closely to develop my own pedagogy for the Luminary training.

Goddess spirituality actively encourages nature knowing, through experiences in the natural world. It reclaims and honours women's ways of knowing, neglected or dismissed within patriarchy, but kept going and passed on for thousands of years. Women's wisdom was banished to folkways yet is emerging in powerful ways today. The wise ways of knowing include herbs, healing, sacred birthing, scrying, oracling, tasseomancy, womb healing, blood mysteries and divination.

Dreams that are memorable, clear and significant are a meaningful way of knowing for many people.

* * *

I have continually developed myself and have explored many intelligences, particularly emotional intelligence (EI) and spiritual intelligence (SQ). Plenty has been written about the discovery that EI is 80% more important than IQ for leadership. Goleman made emotional intelligence mainstream and popular. Of his books, I like *Working with Emotional Intelligence* (1998) best.

In 2001, I wrote an article, 'Emotional Intelligence: The Hidden Advantage' (Sedgmore, 2001), which explained how EI could be of huge value, a hidden advantage even, for college leaders. With 50 other college principals, I had my EI measured on the Hay scale and scored very highly.

More recently, spiritual intelligence has entered the discourse. High EI is considered a prerequisite for SQ. From 2004, I began explorations into SQ and discovered the work of Danah Zohar and Ian Marshall (2000), who describe SQ as "the intelligence with which we access our deepest meanings, values, purposes and highest emotions". They provide a moral and motivational framework with 12 characteristics.

In *SQ21: The Twenty-One Skills of Spiritual Intelligence* (2012, p. 30), Cindy Wigglesworth developed her SQ model, which measures and defines SQ as "the ability to behave with wisdom and compassion, while maintaining inner and outer peace, regardless of the circumstances", and as the integrating intelligence that guides all other intelligences. Her model has 21 skills in an assessment model that can be assessed and intentionally developed. I undertook her assessment in 2012 and evidenced a wide range of SQ capabilities.

I encourage you to expand your ways of knowing and self-awareness and to find an approach that really inspires you.

Reflection

1. Which ways of knowing are you good at?
2. Which ways are more difficult for you?
3. Which might you develop more fully?
4. Which might be fun to explore?
5. How is your emotional intelligence?
6. How is your spiritual intelligence?

Neuroscience and Leadership

This involves understanding how our brains can help us to be more effective and self-aware leaders.

I want to explore our minds from a broad understanding and perspective of what the mind is, not just the rational part. I have studied neuroscience and have learned how our brains are more integrated and interconnected than I had previously thought.

For years, I avoided any study of the brain as too technical and boring. Yet the way in which brain studies have become relevant to leadership now fascinates me. If you have an immediate shut-off reaction to a section about the brain, sit for a while and reflect; see what it's bringing up for you.

Understanding the dynamics of the brain offers fresh and significant insights into human behaviour and shows how we can be more self-aware and able to create environments that support growth and safety rather than unsettle or constrain us. If we want others to thrive, understanding the brain can help. Different studies of neuroscience and leadership offer different conclusions: some say women's and men's brains are different; others say they are mostly similar. Ultimately, it's for you to choose what feels real and true for you.

I am persuaded by two books that have particularly influenced my thinking: *The Gendered Brain: The New Neuroscience*

That Shatters the Myth of the Female Brain (Rippon, 2019) and *The Neuro Edge: People Insights for Leaders and Practitioners* (Hyland, 2017). Both are clear and provide evidence that there are no fundamental differences between the brains of men and those of women.

Neuroscience tells us that we each have three brains. The one we most often think about and pay attention to is the head, or cephalic brain. We also have a heart, or cardiac brain, plus a gut, or enteric brain. Each has sensory neurons, motor neurons, ganglia and neurotransmitters that take in information, process it, store it and access it when needed. Understanding your brain helps you to access different ways of knowing in decision-making, not only being able to trust your head and rationality, but also your intuition and gut instinct, as well as your heart and emotions.

Each of the three brains has a fundamentally different form of intelligence and different goals.

Our cephalic brain is great for thinking, cognitive perception and making meaning of things. At its best, it is the seat of vision, creativity and planning. Our gut brain is designed to focus on our sense of self, on self-preservation and actions. It is the root of our courage and enables us to take any difficult actions necessary. Our heart brain involves emotional processing and fuels our passion and motivation. It keeps us involved, committed, compassionate and connected to our values and relationships with others.

Our brains are the interface between the inside and the outside, an energy system, always learning and responding to our environment. Apparently, it's not too much of an exaggeration to say that the brain is the most complex system in the universe. Being human and acting in the world involves filtering all our experiences, from the moment we are born, through our brains. I was excited to learn that our brains are always learning and actively responding to the environment.

They are what is termed plastic: constantly rewiring with new neural connections being formed and reformed all the time. Our brains constantly enable new behaviours and even the most entrenched behaviours can be modified at any age. This explains why development and spiritual disciplines and practice are all *so* important. We can significantly change our brains, thereby changing our behaviours.

* * *

I want now to look at two practical ways in which integrating the intelligence of our three brains is valuable.

Vision

Since air is the featured element in this Cycle, let's explore the importance of vision. Much has been written about visioning in the leadership literature of the past 20 years. The field of leadership has moved from a more scientific perspective to being seen more as an art. I am fascinated by the inclusion of language once considered religious or spiritual. Today, leaders are expected to have a vision, state a mission, be inspirational and have strong articulated values and be of good or authentic character. This is part of the reason I have developed a leadership formation process that encourages integration of spirituality and leadership. I use the lens of Goddess for all the reasons set out in Chapter 2.

Creating a vision involves forming a picture in your brain, evoked through words or images. I have been involved in many organisational vision creations. Often, we all drew a visual picture with paints and crayons of the individual vision we had, then synthesised them to co-create a shared vision. Visioning can cohere members of a collective around a common vision which everyone can relate to and work towards. A vision is a reference point, providing direction and purpose. Listen to and watch the video of Dr Martin Luther King's famous 'I Have a Dream' speech.[25]

When we do this together on the Luminary course, there is never a dry eye. I have heard this speech countless times, yet it always moves me deeply. Why?

It is a magnificent example of a clear, compelling and emotionally moving vision. It doesn't have any facts or figures or details yet creates a clear image and picture of hope. It connects us to our sense of injustice and desire for things to be better. It provides clear images of what life will be like when his dream is achieved. The speech connects to all three parts of our brain. Our head brain enjoys the clarity of words and images. Our heart brain is deeply affected; we feel emotionally connected and our compassion is aroused. Our gut brain feels motivation, drive and the courage to act towards making the world a better place. We tap into our need to thrive and be safe when the dream is achieved. When our instincts are positively engaged and our emotions and limbic brain system kick in, it gives us the energy to do whatever needs to be done to work towards the vision to which we feel connected.

This is a microcosm of how visioning works. When done authentically, in a way that involves all three brains, it can be a very liberating and powerful experience.

Reflection

1. Listen to the speech and notice how you are affected, and where.
2. Can you identify your different brains being stimulated?
3. Which one is most affected?
4. Do you have a vision that you would like to manifest in the world?
5. Does this section stimulate you to explore neuroscience for yourself?

Supporting the Potential of Others

Significant work has been done on how leaders can foster 'thrive environments'. The brain experiences community primarily as a social system. The same neural responses that drive us towards food or away from predators are triggered by our perception of the way we are treated by other people. People who feel betrayed, unrecognised or diminished experience this as a neural impulse, as powerful and painful as a blow to the head. Most people who work in collectives learn to rationalise or temper their reactions to stay safe but may reduce their commitment and engagement. Leaders who understand this dynamic can more effectively engage the best talent, support collaborative teams and create an environment that fosters productive change. Leadership is always relational, a complex web of perceptions, understandings, misunderstandings, insights and reactions swirling around in the collective.

One of my first Luminary students, Marion van Eupen, expanded David Rock's Scarf model, in one of her assignments, into her Sacred model, which I now use.[26]

These models identify the key social concerns that drive human behaviour and affect the brain. They enable leaders to minimise the threat response and foster a positive response. Where the Scarf model has five qualities – status, certainty, autonomy, relatedness and fairness – the Sacred model has six Luminary qualities that foster a safe environment, with positive leadership behaviours and shadow behaviours for each:

Significance: being valued, seen, heard, recognised and respected

Autonomy: being empowered and trusted, having independence, freedom, choice and creativity

Clarity: having transparency, clear communication, integrity and understanding

Relationship: feeling connection, compassion, rapport, trust,

support and affection
Fairness: perception of fair exchanges between people
Equilibrium: time to vision, play, rest, recharge and meditate
Diversity: equality, fairness, no favourites, participation, inclusion and identity.

The Sacred model provides a means of bringing conscious awareness to potentially fraught interactions and helps to alert you to people's core concerns: ones they may not even understand themselves. It shows how you can consciously co-create a safe and thriving environment for everyone. Every action you take, as a leader, and every decision you make either supports or undermines the perceived levels of these six qualities. This is why leading is so complex. Every word and glance is fraught with social meaning. People experience negative feedback as an attack on their 'significance', which, to the brain, is perceived like a physical attack. Attacks are always met with some kind of defensive strategy. Your sentences and gestures are noticed and interpreted, magnified and combed for meanings you may never have intended.

Reflection

1. When do you feel safe or threatened?
2. How does the Sacred model affect you?
3. How can you foster safety and thriving in your community?
4. What could enable you to foster high engagement and healthy community?

Not Knowing
Older leadership perspectives, particularly the heroic one, advocated that knowing everything is what leaders have to do. This makes any form of not knowing an unacceptable space for

leaders to occupy. In some spiritual traditions, not knowing, the void or Keats's 'negative capability', is actively cultivated.[27]

In Goddess spirituality, not knowing involves deep trust, allowing creativity to arise from the web and matrix of life, as well as seeing and accepting the complexities. When the obvious or linear way forward is neither possible nor desirable, Luminaries know and understand circling and spiralling, staying open to ambiguity, paradox and the unexpected. They enjoy co-creating with others and staying connected to our three brains. They allow the unknown to be birthed into possibilities we could never have imagined in advance. In Spiral 2, we go deep into holding energetic collective space in groups to foster emergence and expansiveness.

I encourage you to explore not knowing; a useful source is *Not Knowing: The Art of Turning Uncertainty into Opportunity* (D'Souza and Renner, 2014). The capacity to feel comfortable about not having all the answers is helped by being a skilled maieutic listener and questioner. As is being able to move with emergence and flow as explored in Cycle IV.

Reflection

1. How comfortable, or not, are you in the place of not knowing?
2. How might you improve your listening and questioning skills?

Synchronous

She is Air and the Wind. She is the Movement of the Invisible. She is Breath. She is Idea and Inspiration...Air is the element that connects us to each other.
Kathy Jones (2006, pp. 102–3)

The literal meaning of 'synchronous' is existing or occurring at the same time, in parallel, concurring or coexisting. It can include the sense of synchronicity, as both involve interconnectivity and things happening at the same time. Synchronous within the Luminary Leaderful Way involves everyone leading simultaneously and recognising more than one leader functioning at the same time. Leaderful is a plural, collective, collaborative and cooperative endeavour, not an individual one. People work together interconnectedly, as peers, with clear roles and accountability.

To be truly synchronous, everyone willingly and consciously shares power with one another. In today's complexity, it can be limiting for there to be only one leader recognised at any one time, holding all or most of the power, until replaced by the next heroic hierarchical authority. A single leader can generate only so many ideas and concentrate on only so many things. A critical mass of leaders allows for more possibilities and more solutions and ideas to be generated. These can be filtered and considered by the group to foster more sophisticated, and better, answers to complex situations. Multiple leaders ensure that everyone can have an input to and influence on decisions, each one contributing their competence, willingness, passion, experience, talents and capabilities. In a Luminary Leaderful mindset, anyone can step up to serve the needs of the collective. Leadership and power is shared, distributed, moves around, is handed over, then picked up again in the collective dance.

Exercise

One of the most popular exercises on the course is manifesting a collective murmuration together as a group. If you don't know what a starling murmuration is, watch a video to see one in action. You can swirl and swarm alone, but the purpose of this exercise is to do it in a group, then to see what happens. Perhaps you can do it with some friends, colleagues or others you know are reading this book. I have adapted the exercise by Rivera Sun in the face-to-face course.[28]

Reflection

1. Explore synchronous and what it means for you.
2. How have you experienced synchronicity in your life?
3. Consider to what extent leadership is an individual or collective experience for you.
4. Practise being spontaneous at least once every day.
5. If you did the murmuration exercise, journal how that felt and what you learned, especially if you were able to do it in a group.

Embodiment Practice

Smudge yourself with a sage stick, or use a feather to smudge yourself with incense, or air.

Clearing Conversations

Another key tool of the Luminary is the clearing conversation, and all my students learn how to do this skilfully with each other. The clearing conversation is a process for two people to come together to discuss their relationship from the perspective of understanding and clearing any issues that have arisen. It involves coming to individual and mutual clarity about where the two of you are in relation to each other. The purpose is genuinely a clearing, to clear the air, to clear the past and to prevent it from accumulating in the future. It may clarify unresolved issues or conflicts, whatever is arising between the two of you. Clear means that you each understand the other as well as possible and this understanding supports working and being with each other more effectively and with more ease.

The focus is on exploring, sharing and clarifying the nature of your relationship without any venting, judging, interpreting, reactivity, blaming or giving advice. Identifying and clarifying whatever is muddy, rusty, unclear, constricting, conflicting, blocking or painful between the two of you. Clearing happens through real, honest, authentic, sincere, open and direct sharing. It can support grappling with any difficulty, conflict, confusion and wounding in the relationship. If you can, try to clear any reactivity: positive transference as well as negative transference. It is not necessary to feel good or friendly or warm, but it is very important to feel clearer with each other and to leave the clearing conversation with your relationship in a more honest, authentic, connected, open and truthful place.

How to carry out the conversation

1. Agree a length of time for the conversation before you begin and honour the agreed time.
2. Take time to *be* present and centred before beginning.
3. If you choose, smudge each other in presence.
4. Bow to each other, then have two minutes of silent eye contact *(take more time if you choose).*
5. One person speaks for up to 10 minutes; the other listens. Then the other does the same. Each says what they want to say without the other responding.
6. Then share in an iterative back-and-forth process for the rest of the time agreed.
7. Neither person's contributions should, at any point, become a lengthy monologue.
8. Wait until the other person finishes speaking. Do not dominate or interrupt.
9. Stay present; keep breathing and listen maieutically.
10. Either person can slow the process down or ask for a brief break if they need it.
11. If one person calls for a pause, honour that; otherwise continue until you both feel clear.

12. You can agree to disagree, or to respect your differing views: consensus is not essential.

13. If it is taking longer than expected, with not enough time to finish, or you become stuck, then pause and fix a time to come back to hold another conversation.

14. Together, come to a completion that suits you both, and end gracefully.

Attitude of the Clearing

Goddess knows and holds you both. You are each vessels for Her love, truth and wisdom. Do your best to see your own personality patterns.

Remember to keep present and breathing throughout the conversation.

Use silence as and when it helps you both.

Remain curious about who this person in front of you really is, beyond images, stories, dramas, projections and judgements. Be realistic and open to change your perspective at any point.

Be authentic and sincere in finding out what is true in your relationship. Risk seeing yourself in a new way. Be compassionate and considerate of the other person's state and their capacity to hear you.

Take full responsibility for your own reactions and speak from your highest and deepest truth, as best you can.

Respect boundaries by being clear about your own needs and limits, as well as those of the other person.

Be specific, not abstract or philosophical. Don't interrupt, analyse, judge or tell the other who they are or what they should do.

Be courageous by naming your own challenge, issue, conflict, dissonance, wounding or pain, exactly as you are experiencing it, with full ownership that it belongs to you.

Do not discharge or emote as it doesn't help to pour everything out in the form of emotional dumping. If you experience gaslighting, simply name it. Don't go into a story and all the details. You can work through your discharge of emotions elsewhere.

* * *

Remember the aims are to get clear, not necessarily to feel warm or loving or fully resolved, and to leave the clearing conversation with your relationship in a more honest, authentic, connected, open and truthful place.

New Moon

A new moon marks the first lunar phase and the start of a new lunar cycle. It symbolises new beginnings. People use the energy of a new moon to start on a new project or to reflect on the previous aspects of their life. It's the perfect moon phase to begin your Luminary journey.

Closing Chant

Listen to the 'I Breathe the Air' chant by Jana Runnalls.[29]

Closing Reflection

Now take time to reflect on all you have learned and experienced in this Cycle. Let it integrate within you. Revisit anything you feel isn't yet complete. When you feel ready, in your own time, move into the next Cycle.

Cycle III Igniting Power, Passion and Intuition

Ignitrix

She who knows Her true power in all its forms. Is unafraid of Her magnificence and impact, releases power wisely in herself and others.

Dimensions
Archetype: **Ignitrix**
Direction: **East**
Element: **Fire**
Moon: **Waxing**
Path of Power: **Overview** and **Within**
State of Being: **Autonomous**
Way of Knowing: **Intuition**

Themes
Intuition, Power, Luminary Path of Power, Activist Leaders

Introduction

To be a fulltime priestess is still a rare profession in these times, to be a priestess Luminary probably even rarer. Still, it makes sense if you realise that the biggest part of being a priestess is about being in service, and the way I learned to be a Luminary was to be a servant leader. My leadership is now grounded in power. This was the biggest lesson I learned: that power does not have to mean hierarchical 'power over'; power does not have to be corrupt either. Power is strongest when it comes from the place of love and from a place of sacredness. To be a priestess Luminary is a to choose a new way of leadership, where both vision and action are in service to Goddess, the Earth and all of Her creation.

Marion, Goddess Luminary

At the east of the Wheel is fire and the archetype Ignitrix: She who knows Her true power in all its forms. Is unafraid of Her magnificence and impact, releases power wisely in herself and others.

This Cycle encourages you to understand and express your own power, to step fully into empowering others and to express Luminary Leaderfulness. An important part of the Luminary teachings is learning to lead effectively in the world as intuitive, passionate Luminaries with a clear and conscious personal relationship with healthy power to ignite and inspire. To help with this, I have created the Luminary Path of Power, which explores types and sources of power, conceptually and experientially. It will enable you to see, understand, access and distribute different sources, types and forms of power for yourself and others. The more you can lead from 'power with' and 'power for', the more liberated you will feel, and the more you will be able to liberate others.

In this Cycle you will:

- experience the clarity and wisdom of trusting your intuition
- let go of all that no longer serves you by releasing and expressing your power in a fire ceremony
- feel the power and potent energy of Goddess and how you can experience your own power
- explore how successful activists and feminists work from their passion for social justice
- understand the oppressive power of patriarchy
- bring your unconscious bias, constrictions and unresolved shadow qualities into awareness for recognition, understanding, feedback, relaxation and letting go
- reflect deeply on your relationship with power and face anything that blocks or diminishes it
- learn all the different sources of power and how you can consciously hold power in a Luminary Leaderful Way.

Feel free (or not) to wear red, orange or pink colour clothes for any part of reading and exploring this Cycle.

Being Present

Before beginning, take time to get present in whatever way suits you best.

Centre yourself, by sitting, standing or walking, indoors or outdoors.

Notice your breathing, your posture and where your attention is. How deep can you go internally? How much is your attention drawn outwards? Go as deep and centred as you can.

Notice your thoughts; can you notice them without being drawn into them?

You may like to begin by lighting a candle and watching the flame. You may choose to light a fire indoors or outdoors. You may wish to drum and dance around or in front of the fire to one of my favourite Goddess power chants, 'Spirits of Fire Come to Us', by Jana Runnalls.[30]

Listen to this chant, or to another you prefer. Feel the words viscerally, repeatedly playing and singing the words until you can feel into and express your own sense of power.

What does it feel like? There is no right way here, only what is right for you.

What sounds (if any) would you like to make? Sing, dance and drum your power.

Take a few moments to reflect on your experience.

For some it is hard to feel your power; others can let go more easily.

Find other power songs and chants that inspire you and foster the expression and release of your power. Two others I particularly like are 'Dancing Fire'[31] and 'Fire Transform Me'.[32]

Calling In

In your own way, call in the element of fire or one or more fire Goddesses. You may want to create an altar and place items on it that say something about your relationship with power you want to share or that help connect you to the element of fire or a specific fire Goddess.

Checking In

Check in with where you are now, before you work through any part of this Cycle; perhaps write in your journal or just notice and be aware of what is happening for you inside and out, here now. Stay as grounded as you can and notice what is happening in your gut. It may help to walk on the land whenever you can.

Intuition

Intuition is being able to understand or to 'get' something instinctively and viscerally, without the need for rational reasoning. It is sometimes called a hunch, a feeling in one's bones, a gut feeling, a sixth sense, or an inkling. It's something we know quickly, without the interference of reason. Often, it's a knowing that's not in the head, yet is significant and real. It's an invaluable internal guidance system which we all have. For some of us, it's hard to locate, even though we experience it. We are taught that the only important way of knowing is through our heads, so we don't learn to hear it, trust it or to act on it.

As explored in Cycle II, we have three brains: one each in our head, heart and gut. Intuition is our gut brain at work, a part of ourselves often overlooked in a culture that overvalues intellect and reason, rating them more important than other forms of knowing. Intuition is a visceral experience when we are in a receptive state to whatever is happening inside us. It is available to everyone, whatever their gender or capacity for conscious self-awareness. It can be easier to experience if we are in an expanded state or deeply present. Connecting to both our intuition *and* our Goddess Gnosis enables us to experience the guidance and wisdom of the deeper intelligence within us.

The reason why we focus on intuition in this Cycle is that you may feel disconnected from or distrustful of your intuition. You may feel unable to differentiate between your gut-knowing originating from fear, or from another internal emotion, and being a deep wisdom that you really need to listen to.

Working with and understanding your intuition can help you differentiate between having an emotional reaction from your personality and experiencing something aligned with your wise, intuitive, authentic self.

Within a patriarchal, male-based, dominator hierarchy power system, most people have become disconnected from their internal, natural, intuitive guidance and power. The power that connects us to our deeper internal wisdom, as well as to our energy, to our Goddess Gnosis. There is huge power, and liberation, if we listen from our bellies and gut, if we trust our own inner knowing, and we allow our intuition to guide us.

In our current, conventional culture and mainstream leadership, intuition is not highly valued. The logical and left-brain approaches of strategising and planning are given priority. Understanding how to tap into our three brains and multiple ways of knowing is important for Luminaries, including our intuition. This enables us to lead from a more integrated and aligned space. The Luminary Way encourages the development, expression and integration of both logic and intuition so that you can draw on either or both, as and when appropriate to your specific situation.

Embodiment Practice

This exercise will encourage you in developing a relationship with, trust in and expression of your own intuition.

1. Close your eyes. Take three deep breaths.
2. Bring to your awareness a time or situation in your life when you relied on your gut feeling, your intuition, when you trusted your inner voice, your sixth sense. It may have felt irrational, but it turned out to be one of the best decisions you have ever made or actions you have undertaken: something that felt true even though it was beyond your intellectual understanding.
3. Recall that moment; take another breath. Really feel into what it felt like at that time.
4. How did your body feel when you made that decision?
5. How did that one decision play a positive role in where you are today?
6. Journal your insight.

Power

Power is mine. I have come to claim it.
Lucy Pearce (2016, p. 129)

It is important to understand your own personal relationship with power. Many of us have difficulty with the fullest expression of our own power, yet we all have it. Luminary Leadership requires you to become clear about your personal relationship with your own power and about how you manifest your power, positively or negatively. To achieve this, it's important to understand viscerally, not just intellectually, exactly how you relate to and express your power. We need to be aware when we empower or disempower others.

Most women are socialised into believing that they lack power and may be actively disempowered. In *Women & Power: A Manifesto*, Mary Beard (2017) explores the misogyny that has shaped our world, and understanding of power, for centuries. If power is seen as a tool only a few people can wield at a time, within systems designed by and for men, an entire sex is potentially excluded from it. She suggests we think of power as the ability to be effective and to make a difference in the world.

I agree wholeheartedly with this. I think of and experience power as an energising flow of natural energy, something everyone needs to understand, express and learn to regulate and flow. An energy that, in and of itself, is neutral yet can be used in ways consciously chosen to use it. Once you truly understand that every one of us has natural power, and you accept that as a fact, then you can learn how to tap into and release its flow. You become better equipped to draw upon and to use your power to make a positive impact in the world.

As power is everywhere and in everyone, it is a two-sided process in any relationship. The amount of power you have over somebody else is affected by the extent of the power they let you have over them, and vice versa. Somebody else can have only as much power or influence over your behaviour as you let them have.

I have been working consciously with women and power

since the early 1980s, when I began teaching on women-into-management programmes. What struck me most was how difficult and complex it was for women to own and experience their own power. Many felt that they had no power, or they didn't want power, primarily because they had experienced it as a negative or distasteful thing. What I realised eventually is that these women were seeing only through a lens of power as dominance, as power over others or as abuse of power. Power for them was something distorted and painful, something they didn't want for themselves.

Within a patriarchal society, power is primarily perceived through the lens of dominance, as this is the philosophy and underpinning of patriarchal power. One sex, the male, is considered superior to all females. Our experience of power, as children, is inevitably influenced by this dominator metaphor and reality, that power is something we have or don't have. We experience that those in control of us, or with more privilege, have more power than we do. It is the unequal distribution of power within patriarchy that helps to maintain the status quo. Those who have power may even be aware of inequities and disparities, but because they fear their own loss of power are unable, or unwilling, to share power and to redistribute it in more equitable ways.

As a feminist in the 1970s and 1980s, I discussed endlessly and earnestly with other women about how we wanted to use our power differently and how important it was to empower each other and to co-create new ways of being together and leading as feminists. We experimented with being leaderless, with circles in which no one person was allowed to be 'the boss'. We were committed to using power benignly, collectively and consensually. It wasn't easy, yet I learned much through those ups and downs. An interesting paper on power and leadership, *The Tyranny of Structurelessness*, by Jo Freeman, instigated an invaluable debate on how denial of the existence of leadership can lead to a different kind of tyranny: one that arises out of a lack of structure.[33]

Freeman argued that a structure, formal or informal, always exists; and to pretend otherwise masks where power lies. Her paper provided a clear rationale for the necessity of explicit transparent structures and processes that do not deny the importance of stepping into leadership roles and influenced me to learn how to explicitly foster shared power, autonomy, engagement and leadership from everyone. This was the beginning of my personal leadership and feminist journey to Leaderful. In *The Empowerment Manual: A Guide for Collaborative Groups* (2011, p. 151), Starhawk furthers this discussion through exploring issues that arise for women working in women-only groups:

> In leaderful...groups...we can create powerful zones of action where many people can become effective agents of change. All of us can be respected and rewarded for our contributions, supporting one another...to act, to confront, to create, to change and, ultimately, to transform the world around us.

This is the feminist utopia we were all aspiring to. I still am.

Metaphors of Power

I have found that exploring power through metaphor can be helpful. As a noun, power is traditionally thought of as the ability or capacity to do something or act in a particular way. From a leadership perspective, power is often described as the capacity to direct or influence the behaviour of others or a course of events. Leaders can be felt as empowering or disempowering; you know it when you experience either. To empower is to give someone else permission, authority or freedom to do something. To disempower is to take someone's power away, leaving them feeling restricted or diminished.

Power as a verb, to power, brings in an association with energy. Conventionally, power is treated like money currency, something you acquire, hold on to or give out to others. I see Luminary power as an energy, more like water or electricity, a neutral energy that exists and flows in everyone, something we are all born with. Luminaries recognise, own and tap into this power in themselves, learning how to use their natural power for the greater good, uploading, releasing, distributing, surging and sharing power wisely and benignly.

I have seen the significant breakthroughs my Luminary students experience when they really understand, on a visceral level, that power is a flow of energy, something they were born with, a natural and neutral force that they already have. I have witnessed their liberation and newfound potency to consciously make choices about how to access their power and use it, knowing it is always there, always available. Yes, you may have had your power diminished, you may have felt cut off from your power, but you can always find it, and draw upon it again.

My Personal Relationship with Power

The simplest and most basic meaning of the symbol of Goddess is the acknowledgment of the legitimacy of female power as a beneficent and independent power. A woman who echoes Ntozake Shange's dramatic statement, "I found God in myself and I loved her fiercely," is saying, "Female power is strong and creative." She is saying that the divine principle, the saving and sustaining power, is in herself.
Carol P. Christ (1992, pp. 273–287)

I have always been preoccupied with the use and abuse of power. Even as a child, I would challenge my father's authority, insisting that he had to earn my respect, not expect it as head of the household simply because of a familial hierarchy based on him being a male. I learned later in life that this power relationship was true of patriarchy within the wider society, not just my own working-class home, and my life as the daughter of a Welsh miner. While being very traditional, my father was also a loving and kind man. He left enough space for me to feel powerful and defiant, as well as disempowered at times, within our stormy relationship. I know this has helped me to develop a healthy relationship with power, but I have had to do lots of work on this theme over many years.

I became an active feminist from the age of 17. I have explored issues of power as a working-class female since I can remember. I was a fulltime activist during second-wave feminism from 1978 to 1982, strongly involved in a range of campaigns. I started fulltime work in further education colleges in 1980. I experienced numerous examples of abusive and toxic use of power. I also taught on women-into-management courses, so was able to explore women and power in depth, experientially and theoretically.

I was promoted to a senior management role at 30, so issues of hierarchical power, and how I worked with power, became very real. I led overtly with feminist principles and supported dozens of women to step into their fullest potential as female leaders. I was frequently the first or only woman in a senior position in a team of men. When I became a senior leader, I knew I had to explore what it meant *not* to be a toxic leader and to find my own style and way of leading. I also felt a strong need to integrate my spirituality into my professional leadership expression. Working in colleges over 36 years, I found the courage to do what I felt was right and to lead autonomously, and collectively, within an ever more centralised and privatised further education system, faced with political and educational policies that were seriously disempowering.

In taking up formal leadership positions, I had to work through my own resistance to taking my own power. I learned the importance of what Starhawk calls keeping power circulating and passing it on. Exactly as she describes, I saw power concentrating in key individuals, and even those leaders I considered to be benevolent and empowering began unconsciously to hoard or abuse power over time. As a feminist, I never wanted that to happen to me. To that end, I worked consciously, as a leader, to explore benevolent power, values and virtues. That included working on my own narcissism, toxicity, shadow and wounding so that I could be more effective, benevolent and non-toxic myself. You will go deeper into toxic leadership in Cycle V.

As a natural-born rebel, who moved into formal and senior leadership positions at an early age, I was able to explore ways in which I could encourage the importance of constructive dissent and the challenging of traditional, hierarchical leadership. As mentioned earlier, my journey is articulated in my professional doctorate (Sedgmore, 2013).[34]

It is also written up in a book about my work (Fry and Altman, 2013) and in a doctoral thesis about my leadership at Guildford College (Joseph, 2002).[35] In a section devoted to 'power, influence and spirituality', Joseph considered the impact – actual and perceived – of my use of power as a leader. The word 'empowerment' was used frequently by others to describe my leadership style; he also commented that I drew more frequently on 'power with' than on 'power over'. He observed that I used a high level of positional and personal power which were "deployed in a benevolent and cooperative way" (p. 182).

My experience is that power over, and tendencies towards domination or toxic power, don't exist only in mainstream organisations. Confusions about power, and unhealthy use of power, exist within progressive movements too, and in spiritual and radical communities. Inevitably, in a patriarchal society we internalise dominance tendencies and carry them with us, no matter how honestly and deeply we believe in egalitarian principles and values. As products of a society organised around domination, the struggle to create equal power relations is vital.

My extensive learning and experience with my own journey of power has culminated in the creation of the Luminary Path of Power model. An important part of the Luminary teachings is viscerally ascertaining your relationship to power and being clear about how you manifest your own power, positively or negatively, understanding when you empower or disempower others. Let's begin your exploration of power with some exercises and a fire ceremony.

Exercise

1. Study the Stages of Living Your Power:
   - Denying
   - Ignoring
   - Suppressing
   - Owning
   - Allowing
   - Comfortable with
   - Expressing
   - Flowing power for others in service
   - Celebrating
2. How does it affect you?
3. Where are you on the list?
4. Circle it; you can circle more than one.
5. Then mark and explore which stage you most want to work on and reflect in your journal.

Exercise

1. Now turn to reflecting on any blocks to power you may be experiencing.
2. Sit still and allow yourself to feel, and name, any blockages to your power, ways in which you let your power be diminished, blocked or extinguished. You might like to write them down in your journal.
3. Now consider any blocks you are ready to let go of to reclaim your full power.
4. Write anything you want to name on paper; use one piece of paper for each word or sentence.

Fire Ceremony

1. Do this ceremony alone or with others.
2. Light a fire outside somewhere where you feel safe and uninhibited.
3. One way to experience your power directly through your gut is by chanting.
4. Play and sing a Goddess fire chant. I really like to get going with 'Dancing Fire' by Jana Runnalls.[36]
5. As you sing and move around the fire, feel the words viscerally.
6. Repeatedly play and sing the words. Make any noises that come naturally.
7. Let your energy build up until you can feel into and express your own power.
8. When you are ready, put your pieces of paper into the fire, one at a time. Name each one aloud and take your time to really feel into what it means, and how it affects you to genuinely let the thing you are naming go. Make sounds, say words: whatever helps you.

* * *

9. Give thanks for your letting go and offer a prayer of gratitude.
10. When you feel complete in this ceremony, close it.
11. Then journal about your experience and any insights you have gained about you and power.

Luminary Path of Power

We have power within us and we have to surface it and step into it.
Geraldine M. Bown (2017b, p. 113)

You now explore various types and sources of power. I have put them into a new model (Figure 4), which has four sources of power; four ways of flowing power when you are with others; six forms of healthy power; and three shadow or toxic forms of power.

Let's go through the model in detail so that you can become conscious about the different ways of holding, understanding and expressing power. Students have found this way of exploring power exciting, revealing and liberating.

Sources of Power

At the centre is fire and Goddess power, the elemental and transpersonal powers of the universe, available to you at all times if you can tap into them.

Presence Power

You explored presence in Cycle I. Now you look closely at the deep power that you can experience in presence. You are present when you can be fully in the moment, deeply centred here now. You can experience Goddess directly and respond

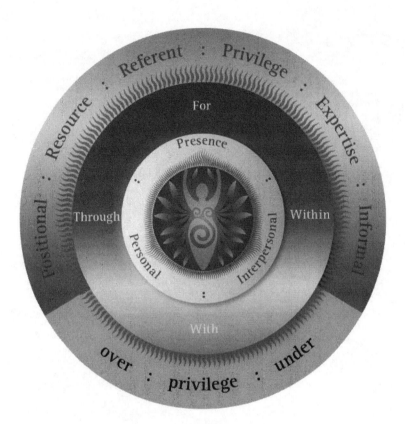

Figure 4 Luminary Path of Power

appropriately to whatever happens, however challenging, easy or unexpected. You have an unshakable and stable power that allows you to be strong and flexible, as well as responsive to others, and clear, in your own viewpoint. In being directly and viscerally connected to Goddess, your presence affects others in a powerful way. The palpable power of presence can be felt by others, enabling them to feel into their own presence and power. When you are directly tuned in and connected to the power of Goddess, you don't take power, or want power, because you *are* power; without arrogance, apology or diminishing anyone else. You hold power through, with, and for others because you want everyone to manifest their own power and autonomy.

Interpersonal Power

This is the power that flows between you and other people. This is your relational power: how you use your power within relationships. People with healthy interpersonal power enjoy peer relationships of mutual respect, and of equals, rather than controlling or dominant ones. Being able to influence is an important interpersonal power, if it's used in a healthy, non-manipulative manner. Leadership is relational, so being clear about your interpersonal power and your own emotional wisdom is important.

Reflection

1. How do you hold power with other people?
2. Do you give it up? Do you let other people dominate you?
3. What is your relationship with power with different people in your life?
4. How effective are you in influencing others in a cooperative and healthy way?

Personal Power

To genuinely experience personal power, you need to feel it and to own it. Ultimately no one can give you power or take it away. It is important to have a strong and visceral connection to, or sense of, your own personal power. Your personal power is strongly linked to your self-esteem and self-worth. As you develop your authenticity, your personal power will flow. You can fully manifest power from within only if you have understood, owned and can stay connected to your personal power. It is important to know your own personal power, regardless of the views or actions of anyone else towards you.

Reflection

1. Do you experience yourself as a powerful person or not?
2. How would you describe your sense of personal power, or lack of it?

Ways of Flowing Power

Power For

This involves consciously choosing to use your power for others. It is also called 'power on behalf of'. The aim of power for is to use your power in the interests of the people you serve, support or ally with. It involves helping others find and express their own power, without creating dependency.

Using power in this way is particularly important if you are working with oppressed or marginalised individuals and groups who may have been disempowered by consistently having their power diminished or taken away. People who are traumatised, wounded or disconnected from their own power may turn to someone with privilege, and healthy power, to support them. It is important when drawing on this form of power not to fall into saviourism, hubris or arrogance; or to indulge a feeling that you are superior, in any shape or form, to the people on whose behalf you are working.

Who might you offer your power on behalf of?

Are you clear how to do this without hubris?

Power Within

This is the power that you have direct access to from inside yourself, the direct visceral knowing of your own power. This is the power that you were getting in touch with during the fire ceremony. Power within stems from really knowing who you are and being your authentic self; knowing that you are power and that you have everything you need from within. Power is an energy residing in all of us, including you. Accessing your power is threaded throughout the Luminary teachings and exercises in direct and more subtle ways.

Reflection

1. How do you know your inner power directly and viscerally?
2. What happened in the fire ceremony?
3. If you are uncertain about your own power within, talk to someone who feels clear and confident in their own power within.

Power With

Power with is a conscious desire to share power with others. It is also called 'shared power', as it involves sharing power with others. You need to be confident in your own power to be able to share it with people you are working with on a task, project, situation or process. It involves co-creating together, as peers and equals, sharing your power by drawing on one another's talent, skills and expertise, as appropriate to the context. Leaders who are comfortable working from power with can co-create processes and policies that genuinely empower everybody. They initiate and encourage collective processes and a peer culture. They resist being the individual heroic leader or the one who has all the answers. They encourage conversations, challenges, deep discussions, and have a genuine authentic respect for everyone, including themselves.

Reflection

1. How have you shared your power with others?
2. How did it feel?
3. Have you had experience of someone sharing their power with you?

Power Through

This is the place of power where you don't need to be seen, to be visible or at the forefront. You are clear that you have power, and you choose to use it to inspire and encourage others to know their own power and to feel powerful. You may yield this power from behind by being in the background while facilitating, enabling, supporting, coaching, advocating, allying and finding all kinds of ways in which you enable others to step into their power. In this space, you don't give your power away: you are sharing and offering your power through others. For some, this space of power comes later in life when you have gained more wisdom or expertise or don't need to be in the limelight or to gain significance any more, but it can happen at any stage of life. Power through is important to foster the individual and collective empowerment of as many people as possible, as a far more effective and powerful way forward than any one person on their own can manifest.

Reflection

1. When have you worked with power through? How did it feel?
2. What action can you take to support and encourage healthy power relations within the community or organisation you work in?

Healthy Power

Positional Power

The power of position is power gained from holding a particular position or role in a community or organisation. Formal positional power is the primary way of holding power in traditional dominator hierarchies. The closer you are to the top of the pyramid, the broader the scope of your authority and your influence on decision-making, and on other people. Peer communities of equals distribute positional power by holding accountability in clearly articulated and collectively agreed roles, and in circles, rather than through traditional hierarchical structures. It is an exciting time in leadership of moving into more equitable and collectively accountable ways of leading. The way in which you use your formal positional power will vary depending on your unique relationship with power.

Reflection

1. How have you used any positional power you have held?

Resource Power

This is about the resources you can access, control or give out, related to the impact they have on others. Resources can include the ability to give reward of varying kinds, such as performance bonuses and flexible working, or the size of financial budget you hold. In education, a major resource power is timetabling, access to photocopying, stationery and technology equipment, or room usage. The power in having resources lies in being able to give, withhold or restrict these resources. In some organisations, some positional roles have 'resource' in their title.

The effectiveness of resource power, particularly monetary reward, is related to its congruence with the perceived value and significance of the reward by those receiving it. In a healthy way, reward is about giving something in recognition or appreciation of achievement or effort. Unhealthy reward power can be used manipulatively and for the wrong reasons. The overuse of resource power by a leader may foster purely transactional relationships.

Reflection

1. How have you used any resource power you held?

Referent Power

Referent power lies in the respect we have for another person. Such power is given explicitly or implicitly, formally or informally, but only through willing consent. It can occur immediately or slowly, and cannot be taken, only given. It is offered to people who are seen as legitimate, valued, trustworthy and competent, *not* because they hold a formal position. Often, successful leaders with well-known track records of success are given referent power as they are well respected, liked and trusted. You may feel inclined to work harder for someone whom you like or admire, because you may want their approval and acceptance. If it is gained through showing genuine concern and demonstrating respect for others, referent power can be encouraging and empowering. People feel comfortable and motivated in the presence of leaders on to whom they refer power. If a leader lacks integrity or becomes overly narcissistic, referent power previously given may be withdrawn.

Reflection

1. Have you ever received referent power?
2. If so, how did it feel and how did you use it?

The Power of Conscious Privilege

Privilege means having some kind of benefit, right or exemption, simply because of the colour of your skin, your sex or the family or place you were born into. It includes all the advantages and power held by you, as an individual, or as part of a group, who are in the majority. You can have privilege in any of the following: ability, sex, race, class, sexuality, age, health, gender identity, religion, economic wealth, education and accent. You can have privilege in one aspect while being oppressed in another. Having privilege does not mean you have had an 'easy' life or have never faced discrimination: it means that in our social system you are afforded more rights or privileges than others. This has inherent power within it, even if the privileged person cannot see that fact. While you cannot get rid of your privilege, there is no need to feel shame or guilt; the key is to see and understand the nature of the privilege you have, and to find ways of using that privilege to support those who don't have it.

Bringing awareness of your privilege out of your unconscious is an important journey to undertake. The purpose of knowing your privilege is to ascertain how you can use it to support and liberate others, especially those experiencing more oppression than you. Use your privilege to be an ally to individuals and groups who don't share your privilege. Owning your privilege means you do not attempt to step in the way of another person asking for more rights; instead, you use your privilege to lift their voice, without needing thanks. A more privileged person is more likely to be listened to within the system.

Using your privilege can include giving your time, money, energy, literacy, mobility, connections, housing and travel opportunities. Many baby boomers are using their economic privilege to donate to social movements, paying for young people to attend courses they otherwise could not afford, supporting charities, or giving their time, unpaid, to add value to individuals or groups through advocacy work, lobbying, campaigning, protesting and organising. Younger people are using their technological and educational privilege to boycott organisations, companies and politicians through social media and spending their money on organisations that not only align with their values but also publicly ally with minority groups.

My personal privilege is being white, being married, being

educated to postgraduate level, and having good health, physical ability and financial stability. I own my own home and have a final salary pension. Being a baby boomer gives me significant social and economic advantages. I use my privilege to offer free or reduced-cost coaching, low-cost leadership development, healing and financial support to young women entrepreneurs, as well as microlending to women in many different countries. I contribute to many charities. I have had to educate myself and do deep inner work to see my privilege. It was much easier to see my oppressions, as a woman from a poor, working-class council estate. My class identity is still working class as I am enormously proud of my roots. To keep in touch with my origins, I visit my primary school every year to give an award and cheque to a pupil, in the name of my father. Setting up this award was a way of coping when he died unexpectedly in 1997.

Reflection

1. Really think about who you are and what your privilege is.
2. Clarify and list your privileges.
3. Look at any entitlement, privilege or oppression in your lineage.
4. Which privilege or privileges can you draw upon to support others?
5. Which aspects of your privilege are you willing to use, and how?
6. Who can you approach to see if they would welcome your allyship?
7. Co-create with them a list of actions they would like you to support them with.

Expert Power

Expert power derives from your level of expertise. It is granted to people who have reputable and proven experience, skills or knowledge. It can take the form of in-depth, specialist information, technical skill or role expertise required in a particular context. It may also be something acquired from years of experience, such as knowing how to traverse community or group dynamics in a skilful way, or knowledge of networking links. It may be related directly to the role held or can be an expertise acquired in a personal capacity that becomes needed. Expert power derives from acceptance that a person possesses appropriate or superior skills, knowledge and abilities. Expert power works best when balanced with wisdom and humility without any exaggeration of the extent of the expertise.

My fascination with and in-depth knowledge of different faith traditions became a powerful expert power after the London bombings in 2006, when the government was keen to introduce faith literacy. I was able to create a faith literacy toolkit within a few weeks to launch at the East London Mosque, because of this personal expert power.

Reflection

1.   How have you used any expert power you have held?

Informal Power

You don't have to have an official or formal role to be powerful within a collective. Many people are influential and have referent power, even though they don't hold any kind of official leadership role. Their power lies in being seen as valuable, trusted, and as someone who gets things done. They may also be a strong influencer of someone holding a powerful formal role. They may never be recognised as powerful within the formal power system, yet everyone knows who they are within the informal power networks. In every form of grouping, an informal power network exists.

I often found myself as an informal power person when I first worked in junior positions in colleges. I was given referent power and had strong interpersonal power, and developed expert power, very quickly. As a senior formal leader, when I went into new organisations or departments, I would ask "Who are the people who may not be senior but have lots of power and influence around here?" Every time I asked, once they had clarified and trusted that I meant no harm towards them, people named at least six informally powerful people immediately. I would then approach those individuals and ask them to work with me in constructive ways, simply because they were important influencers and held significant power. It frequently came as a surprise to those individuals that they were powerful. Often, informal power people are the rebels, the people who speak out and speak truth to formal power: individuals who are deeply respected and admired throughout the organisation.

Reflection

1. Have you been aware of holding informal power?
2. If so, how did it feel and how did you use it?
3. Did you know who held informal power in your community or organisation?

Unhealthy Power

We need to be able to see, understand and challenge unhealthy, toxic manifestations of our power, especially as leaders, and to understand when we are leading out of our own shadow. In Cycle VI, we explore in depth toxic leadership and our own shadow. What I concentrate on here is describing the different kinds of power that emanate from our unconscious shadow, or our unresolved issues with power.

Power Over

Power over usually derives from having positional power because of a formal role and an authority recognised by others. Most organisations work within power structures that have dominator hierarchies in which positional power, manifesting as power over, is considered the normal and acceptable way of leading. This stems out of the normative dominance in our patriarchal society whereby one person oppresses another. In unusual and extenuating circumstances, such as a major crisis, a conscious choice to draw on power over skilfully may be morally and situationally justified, but only ever as a one-off to take charge and to tell people what to do to get out of danger or to save lives.

Some people feel comfortable expressing power over because this is all they know of power, or because they cannot allow themselves to be anything but strong. These are people who have responded to trauma and abuse of power by deciding never to be a victim, even though they were. This person, at their worst, uses power over in an aggressive way. This is because that is what they have learned from people who held power over them in tyrannical or oppressive ways. These people need to work through their relationship with power to understand and expand into a broader range of power sources.

Reflection

1. In what ways can you create space and conversations to learn various power perspectives and leadership styles that differ from your own (ones that don't use power over)?

2. What action can you take to challenge or disrupt the status quo of unhealthy dominator power relations within the community or organisation you work within?

The Power of Unconscious Privilege

I have included privilege in the unhealthy power section as well as the healthy power one, because unconscious privilege can be deeply harmful. Unless they do the work, people who are members of the majority group and hold a normative perspective will inevitably uphold and ensure the continuation of the status quo. In a patriarchy, that status quo is white, male and heteronormative. Some men, particularly white men, gain benefits and privileges purely by being born male. Privilege is often something the privileged group haven't thought about or cannot see because they have never experienced being oppressed, or don't have sufficient interest or empathy.

At the opposite end, privileged people who choose to be advocates for, or allies of, disadvantaged individuals or groups may do so in a way that is harmful or unhelpful. They may lack the humility and awareness to use their power of privilege to empower others in ways that are wanted. Trying to be someone else's 'saviour' in an egocentric manner, for the wrong reasons, is never a good thing. It is wrong to provide help to marginalised people in a self-serving manner or just to receive some kind of reward. These are all forms of using the power of privilege unhealthily.

Understanding and using the healthy power of privilege, and moving through from unconscious bias to conscious bias, involves doing a lot of work on yourself. It involves actively and consistently challenging, unlearning and re-evaluating your own position of bias, privilege and power.

Conscious bias arises from seeing what has been unconscious within us, and labelling it as an automatic response, honestly witnessing where and how we treat others differently or negatively. Luminaries work tirelessly to see their own conscious and unconscious bias, prejudices and beliefs and proactively stop any behaviours that disrespect or limit others.

Unconscious bias and microaggressions lie in our shadow,

so we need to work actively to reveal them by noticing when and how we treat others discriminatively. They can be changed or interrupted through honest self-exploration, feedback and practice. Unconscious bias consists of the feelings, beliefs and constructs we were taught by our parents, teachers, peers, media and society that remain in our unconscious. We all have cultural influences, constructs and beliefs that create bias, consciously and unconsciously. From an early age we are taught and influenced to categorise and separate people into mental and emotional hierarchies of normality against which we judge and compare people. We are all different and we all carry biases in ourselves and our cultures, each with their own particular flavour. Bias itself is not the issue; it's when bias is used to discriminate, oppress and marginalise that it becomes a problem. In this way, our biases inhibit our ability to judge a person or group in any way other than how we were taught and have internalised. Every day, we meet another person's bias and prejudice as well as exhibiting our own.

When it is left unchecked, unconscious bias can impact the way we lead, communicate and behave in our professional, community and personal lives. If we do not recognise, understand, monitor, control and change our unconscious bias, we may be involved in discriminatory language and behaviour, however much we think we are not. If our bias relates to the protected characteristics specified in our country's equality laws, we could be breaking the law.

This work needs compassion and sensitivity, because shaming, blaming and outing may increase defences rather than dissolve them. Change begins with you and your motivation to change yourself for the better.

In our patriarchal society, our own and other people's biases, privilege and prejudices are everywhere. The more conscious we are, the more we are skilful with our thoughts, actions and the way in which we lead. Becoming more conscious of these systemic dynamics and challenging our assumptions is the first step to addressing them.

'Microaggressions' is a term used for commonplace verbal or behavioural slights that engender hostile or derogatory attitudes towards people from marginalised groups, intentionally or unintentionally. It's the smaller things, daily, which can have a draining and diminishing impact. Examples include deliberately omitting someone from an email; reacting differently to someone's accent, too positively or negatively; speaking too fast, or unclearly, to someone in a language not their primary tongue; and continually mispronouncing names or inappropriately reacting to a name not from your own culture. These sorts of actions can demotivate, create mistrust, generate fear and disempower. Yet too frequently they are not taken seriously, and people affected feel unable to name them. If microaggressions are not interrupted, they become normalised, then institutionalised. Conscious action at personal, team and institutional levels is vital to disrupt these patterns. If all this is completely new to you, you may need support and training from a professional and to attend unconscious bias or cultural awareness training. There are numerous ones available.

Reflection

1. Can you see any ways in which you have privilege and are drawing on it in unhealthy ways?
2. What is your understanding of unconscious bias and microaggressions and the ways they show up in your life and workplace?
3. What actions could you take to recognise and reduce unconscious bias or microaggressions?
4. Do you engage in them yourself?
5. How can you repair or interrupt, in any way you can, your inappropriate actions towards others?

6. Are you on the receiving end of any unconscious bias and microaggressions?
7. How might you create space for discussion, resolution and change with those directly involved?
8. Do you feel able to challenge skilfully any unconscious bias or microaggressions you or others experience?

Exercise

1. Write the names or initials of up to 10 people you really trust (not immediate family).
2. Categorise those people in terms of education, sex, gender identity, age, sexuality, ethnicity, disability and any other qualities that feel important to you. Sameness is safe but may be limiting your horizons. Whatever the profile of your 10, it's not a problem: the point is to be aware of it.
3. Is there a pattern?
4. Do they all look like you or are they different?
5. Does any pattern of having sameness around you affect your decision and choices?
6. How can you get to know and understand people outside your usual experience?

Power Under

I want to explore this in some depth, as I feel it is very important. Steven Wineman developed this concept in *Power-Under: Trauma and Nonviolent Social Change*. His website has resources and more information.[37]

Srilatha Batliwala explores it in *Feminist Leadership for Social Transformation: Clearing the Conceptual Cloud*. She provides illustrations of occasions when power under manifests in feminist and women-only groups, and the learning to be gained.[38]

Power under is the way in which individuals who have experienced significant abuse, oppression and trauma express their power by unconsciously and unwittingly acting in disempowering, abusive or authoritarian ways. It happens because they are unhealed from their trauma and wounding. They are also disconnected from any sense of their own flow of power and energy. They act from an internal state of unconscious powerless rage, while feeling they are being empowering. This can have a hugely negative impact on the person, or group, on the receiving end of this.

Power under can also involve entrenched positions of helplessness, powerlessness, and victimisation, chronic complaints and explosive anger. Those under its grip may become locked into power struggles that cannot possibly be won. They may create splitting into sharply defined figures of benevolence or malevolence, with the utter conviction that they are being acted upon and victimised. Power under is highly susceptible to infighting and splintering, creating difficulties in any efforts to build coalitions of people with multiple identities.

It is important to learn how to honour the integrity, pain and impact of everyone's experiences of oppression and of powerlessness. Patterns of self-abuse and chronic expression of powerless rage are all indicators of unhealed trauma. The trauma and wounding of someone expressing power under needs understanding and support, so they can become more skilful in holding, expressing and manifesting their power in healthy ways.

I wish I had understood power under many years ago. We have language and frameworks to identify problems caused by power over; we also need to find ways to work through power under. I now offer my understanding of the four types of leaders who function primarily from power under.

Read these and see if you have been affected by any of them.

Four Power Under Leadership Roles

I have identified four different ways of expressing power under from my own reading, explorations and experience in different groups and communities.

The complexity and pain in every one of these four positions arises from making power traumatic and very personal. Due to wounding and reactivity, these leaders are unable to see any broader structural oppressions, and that power exists within all collective situations. I hope an understanding of these four forms of expressing power under will help you to understand others better, as well as being better equipped to protect yourself.

1. The victim–oppressor leader

This person, even when they do have the authority and power of leadership, formally or informally, still perceives themselves as a victim. They remain a victim, even when they themselves are behaving in ways that are harming, limiting or oppressing others. If someone tells them that they feel violated, hurt or harmed in some way by their behaviour or use of power, the victim–oppressor is unable to receive feedback in any way, other than as an attack on them personally. Their internal wounding and unhealthy relationship with power translates any feedback that is uncomfortable to them as an attack from the other person, consistently turning themselves into a victim. This can be linked in many ways to the notion of fragility. Much has been written about white fragility and fragility linked to people in privileged roles who haven't enough internal resilience or are not sufficiently self-aware to understand the impact they are having on others. I have experienced this, personally, in a range of groups and communities and organisations. It is exhausting and requires huge emotional labour not to be drawn into the mindset, gaslighting and emotional diminishment of the victim–oppressor. Somehow, they manage to turn reasonable, objective, factual comments and feedback into a perceived abusive attack on their integrity, behaviours, beliefs or understanding.

2. The reluctant–ambivalent leader

This person is resistant or reluctant to own their power or to step into a clear and healthy expression of leadership. They resist any labels or attribution that they are a leader, even if it's clear to everyone else that they hold all the functions and resources of a leader. They can often be heard saying "We're all leaders here", or "I am not the leader", in a context where there are no processes for any kind of shared or distributed leadership. This absolves them of any sense of being held to account, or of consciously exploring, understanding and being a skilful leader. It requires incredible skilfulness and resilience to challenge this person, especially when they feel in their deepest wounding. They lack consistency about when they will step in as leader to control or manage situations that bother them, or not. This can be erratic and confusing to those on the receiving end. They may swing from being your peer to suddenly telling you what to do if they feel stressed, or they start criticising, out of the blue. This can be disempowering and confusing. In a group that desires equality, a peer community of equals, it's the strong personalities who step in and out of authority and can gradually prevent anyone else from having the power to act or create sufficient confusion and demotivation that people leave. When asked to be the leader or to take accountability or offered challenging feedback about their ambivalence or the situation they are creating, the reluctant–ambivalent leader feels threatened, moves into denial and quickly defends themself.

3. The rejector non-leader

This person will not hold a position of formal authority or power and sees anyone who does so as an oppressor and a personal abuser of everyone. They have a serious issue with anyone holding any kind of authority over them. They will do all they can to subvert, oppose and manipulate those who take positions of power. Empowerment for them means always siding with any perceived victim and getting what they want manipulatively. They may gain power by taking the position of victim and making everyone else walk on eggshells. The rejector non-leader focuses their nurturing and attention on others, those who also take the position of victim and consistently complain about anyone holding formal authority. They gain social power, not by taking on responsibility, but by complaining about or resisting those who do.

4. The I-am-not-a-victim–oppressor leader

This person feels comfortable expressing power over because they cannot allow themselves to be the victim. In some ways this is the opposite of the victim–oppressor leader. They have responded to trauma and abuse of power by deciding never to be a victim, even though they were. This person at their worst uses their power over in an aggressive way because that is what they have learned from people who held power over them. They manifest rage and anger in unhealthy ways and are blocked from any compassion for anyone they consider is displaying victim tendencies. The I-am-not-a-victim–oppressor leader will find compassion and acknowledgement for anyone they feel is a victim only when the hurt, injured and wounded part of themselves is given time and attention to seeing and healing their own victim. They need to develop an ease with their power without becoming tyrannical or oppressive, expanding into a broader range of power sources and capacities.

Reflection

1. Can you see yourself or anyone else you know in any of these forms of power under expression?

2. If so, find strategies and support to help you work

through your own healing and to find ways to be in healthy power relationships, as much as is possible.

I offer my list of ways of coping with power under:

- Getting clear on my own relationship with power under
- Observing what others do and finding a way of speaking truth to wounded power
- Understanding power under
- Holding the person exhibiting power under with compassion
- Finding the strength to hold my own boundaries and truth
- Finding my inner resilience, compassion and motivation to challenge in a way I can be heard
- Articulating how I want the person to change their behaviour so that the relationship can continue
- Walking away, if necessary, from the specific situation and the person involved
- Creating safe spaces to listen constructively to each other's stories of violation and oppression
- Working together through our resistances and the issues of power we are experiencing
- Telling and hearing our life stories without self-justification or defence
- Understanding and responding coherently and humanely to the complex intertwining of being in the oppressor and oppressed roles together.

* * *

Now that you have worked through the whole Luminary power model, it is important to integrate your relationship with power. Having felt your power intuitively and through your gut and explored the 17 elements of the Luminary Path of Power, here are seven questions for more personal reflection. This exercise is designed to help you understand some of the ways in which your relationship with power has been shaped by your early experiences of it, then to clarify your current use of and relationship with power. Please take care of yourself if some of the questions are difficult; go only as far as you want to and feel safe enough to explore. Do your best to stay in touch with your feelings throughout.

Exercise

1. Try to remember the first time you became aware of power between people and noticed that some people have more power than others. Try to recall what specifically made you aware of the power dynamic in the interaction. It could be an experience of any of the types of power described in the model above.

2. Try to remember an experience when you felt powerless. What was happening? Who was in control? Why did you feel powerless? How did you feel in your body? What did you do? How did you react?

3. Now, try to recall the first time you became aware of your own power, your power within. What type of power was it? Recall what specifically made you aware of your power in the interaction.

4. Which of the following power positions have you occupied in relationship with others?

    a. **Subjected**: when you were the subject of control (when someone was exercising power or authority over you); how did you feel?

    b. **Equivalence** or **with**: when you were working together with others, exercising joint authority and equal power; how did you feel?

  c. **Over**: when you were exercising power over others; how did you feel?

  d. **Under**: when you expressed or felt power from your wounding; how did you feel?

  e. **Through**: when you felt power coming through you; how did you feel?

  f. **For**: when you drew on your power on behalf of others, and acted out of service; how did you feel?

  g. **Other**: a power relationship other than the above; please explain and then describe how you felt.

5. Which power position have you found yourself in most often?

6. From among these various power positions, reflect honestly which position or positions you are most comfortable with.

7. Now reflect and capture any insights that come from deep within about your relationship to power. How might these insights help you in how you will consciously choose to use power as a Goddess Luminary? What is your most important insight into yourself and power?

8. How do the answers and insight from the questions above help you to understand your leadership more deeply? What it is now and what it might be into the future?

Activist Leaders

I joined the Luminary programme to better understand leadership and my place in it. My uncomfortable relationship to finding my Leaderful way was blocked by preconception imprinted on me by patriarchy. I have been a direct-action campaigner for 30 years yet was still seeing my battles through a subordinate's lens. With Lynne's teachings, I explored and dispelled blocks and binds that made me feel unworthy. As well as being on the front line, I now

run seminars with activists, teaching that they are all leaders in
service to the world and how to come from a strong, centred place.
Indra, Goddess Luminary

Goddess opens eyes, not just to the injustices done to women, but
to all injustice. Our current culture is one where the patriarchy
believes that it has dominion over everything: women, children,
animals, natural resources and the planet. For me, activism has
always been a service and a sacred act. I became an activist
feminist at the age of 17 and was strongly involved in a range
of campaigns. Activism and leadership have been part of my
spiritual journey. Being an activist forces you to ask yourself
how much you're willing to risk and why. How far are you
willing to go to see your dreams come true? What is the price
you're willing to pay? At times you even have to ask what is
worth living or dying for. These are existential questions which
challenge us to go beyond our limited, day-to-day living and
gain a wider view of our purpose in life.

For many, activism is a spiritual practice and a way of life,
wanting a better world, social justice or to save the planet. All
activists are passionate about a particular cause that ignites
their inner fire and motivates them to act. They fight against
oppression and work to overthrow, change or transform
society. Activists are clear about what they are against and what
they don't want in the world. They take part in public protests
and instigate a range of interventions and actions to promote,
impede, direct or intervene in social, political, economic or
environmental reform or change.

The various forms of activism include writing letters, political
campaigns, boycotts, rallies, street protest marches, strikes, sit-
ins and hunger strikes. Activism can include economic activism,
that is, refusing to spend money with companies that exploit
their workers. Most activism involves organising collective
action for large numbers of people to protest together to

make a significant impact. Activists use literature, pamphlets, manifestos, books and social media to disseminate their messages and to facilitate engagement and collective action. Mass action that is well organised and becomes sustainable over time becomes a social movement. Examples of global and new social movements include Black Lives Matter, #MeToo and Extinction Rebellion.

At the heart of activism is opposing all abuses of power. The ways in which activists relate to power and authority range from anarchists through to more conventional groups. Many activists have explored and experimented with practices and ways of sharing power that resist the conventional power dynamics of individualistic, heroic, power over and dominator hierarchies.

From my own study of activists, I have identified key motivations, behaviours, characteristics and shadow characteristics:

Common Motivations and Behaviours

- Are fired and inspired by changing the world for the better
- Move power from the few to the many
- Fight injustice and unfair oppressive systems or people
- Are self-appointed
- Are often outsiders of the establishment
- Want liberation and equality for the oppressed and disadvantaged
- Take direct action through protest
- May use violence, or may oppose it
- Use tactics of strikes, campaigns, obstruction and marches
- Have no respect for traditional authority if considered unjust and oppressive
- Mobilise mass participation on a huge scale
- Attract huge followings.

Characteristics

- Courageous
- Feisty
- Inspiring
- Passionate
- Demanding
- Effective orators
- Unstoppable
- Willing to die to further the cause
- Perseverance in the face of opposition, torture and imprisonment
- Defiant, stay strong in their own truth
- Highly autonomous
- Inspire love and hate (assassinations)
- Innovative.

Shadow Characteristics

- Mercenary
- Sociopathic
- Lack of empathy for anyone or anything beyond their 'cause'
- Obsessed, can rant about their cause
- Unreflective.

Reflection

1. What are you passionate about?
2. Explore how you can manifest your own activism in the world.
3. Are there any social movements you would like to become involved in?
4. Find an activist you can learn from.

Waxing Moon

As the moon waxes, it grows brighter and its illumination becomes fuller as it expands into a full moon. As you truly know your power, you can begin to wax more fully into the world.

Closing Songs

Three songs that really help me to feel into my power are:

- 'A Call to Stand' by Eleonora Brown[39]
- 'I Am Woman' by Helen Reddy[40]
- 'Full Height of Our Power' by Shawna Carol, sung by Kellianna.[41]

Closing Reflection

Now take time to reflect on all you have learned and experienced in this Cycle. Let it integrate within you. Revisit anything you feel isn't yet complete. When you feel ready, in your own time, move into the next Cycles.

Cycle IV The Weave and Flow of Interconnection

Connectrix

She who is conscious of the deep interconnection of all life, who weaves and flows for the greater good of all. Understanding her impact upon others with tender sensitivity and open-hearted compassion.

Dimensions
Archetype: **Connectrix**
Direction: **South**
Element: **Water**
Path of Power: **With**
State of Being: **Adaptive**
Leaderful Way: **Flow**
Way of Knowing: **Heart**

Themes
The Interconnected Luminary, Adaptive, Flow, Service, Connection

Introduction

...the best way to care for ourselves is...To connect with each other in ways that propel all of us toward care – for ourselves and one another.
Alicia Garza (2020, p. 288)

In the south of the Wheel is water and Connectrix: She who is conscious of the deep interconnection of all life, who weaves and flows for the greater good of all. Understanding her impact upon others with tender sensitivity and open-hearted compassion.

In this Cycle, you feel into your heart, into flow, into relationships and the element of water. You experience open-heartedness, your tender heart, your sensitivity and your deep connection with everyone and everything. You will explore the holding, allowing, regulation and expressing of emotions. You explore the notion of service, and whom you want to serve. At its core, leadership is relational. It's all about people, people working together, creating together, being together in connection; *we*, not *I*. An important part of being Luminary and Leaderful involves weaving a dance with others, a dance of relationships, connection and flow. The more you can keep your heart open, know your own emotions and stay open to flow and connection, the more adaptable, responsive and impactful you will be.

In this Cycle you will:

- explore interconnectedness through the Luminary Interconnectedness model
- explore the concepts of flow, service and connection and how to be more skilful in each
- viscerally experience your own flow and how adaptive you are

- be more open to and conscious of leading from your heart
- understand the importance of healthy relationships
- know your impact upon others.

Feel free (or not) to wear blue colour clothes for any part of this module.

Being Present

Before beginning the work for this module, take time to get present in whatever way suits you best. Centre yourself, by sitting, standing or walking, indoors or outdoors.

Notice your breathing, your posture and where your attention is. How deep can you go internally? How much is your attention drawn outwards? Go as deep and centred as you can.

Notice your thoughts; can you notice them without being drawn into them?

You may like to use the Heart Meditation below or begin by listening to Ashana's beautiful song, 'Opening to Love'.[42]

Calling In

In your own way, call in the element of water or one or more water Goddesses: whatever feels 'right' for you. You may want to create an altar and place items to hold you, as you work through the themes. Place items that say something you want to share about your adaptability and relationship with flow, or that help connect you to the element of water or a specific Goddess of water.

Checking In

Check in with where you are now, before you work through any part of this Cycle; perhaps write in your journal or just notice and be aware of what is happening for you inside and out, here now. Please be kind, sensitive and loving to yourself. Place your attention into your heart. What is happening there?

If you want to, read the words below slowly and meditatively:

Heart Meditation

An important part of leadership is to hold an open heart
To be deeply connected to your heart
To remain in touch with the qualities of your heart
To feel love, and to be able to act and lead from love
To become more delicate, more gentle, more vulnerable,
more receptive and more compassionate. Deeply loving.
How can you cultivate your compassion, your vulnerability?
Your gentleness, sensitivity and consideration?
How can you practise kind understanding and valuing of
yourself, of other people and other beings?
Let go of any hardness, toughness, thickness, insensitivity,
criticism, harshness and dullness
Let go of treating yourself or other people critically or
unkindly.
The gentler you are,
the more delicate you are,
the more sensitive you are,
the more vulnerable and compassionate you are,
the closer you are to your heart.
To the reality of your Goddess Gnosis,
directly feeling Her love and your authentic self.

Sit in silence for as long as feels right.
If you choose to do so, reread the passage.
Sit now with how feeling deeply into your heart affects you.
What is happening for you? Notice it, no judgement, just what
is.
Be aware of any sensitivity, delicacy, sweetness, tenderness and
love. Be kind with your heart.

Now, take in noise, listen from your heart, stay in presence and depth.

Gently come back into the room through your heart.

Open your eyes, look from your heart, notice how you see from your heart.

Feel what is happening in your heart now. Really feel into your heart.

The heart leads us home to love. Keeps opening us to love.

How close are you to your own heart? What is arising?

Journal or say something your heart wants to communicate here now.

The Interconnected Luminary

This Luminary Interconnectedness model (Figure 5) is my synthesis of a range of approaches I have studied, experimented with and found useful over many years. It comprises three Wheel dimensions: flow, service and connection, with six facets each.

The overall purpose of the model is to help you to be interconnected, adaptive and resilient in whatever relationship or situation you find yourself in. Some people are better equipped in some of these facets than others. Someone may be particularly skilled at seeing their unconscious bias but could find it difficult to comfort another in a difficult personal situation. Luckily, our brains are incredibly plastic, capable of constantly learning new information and skills, and our relational skills can be developed and improved. As you explore, experience, practise and integrate all the facets, you will be more interconnected in all your relationships. The facets are a mix of intelligences, qualities, attitudes, motivations, actions, skills, states and experiences.

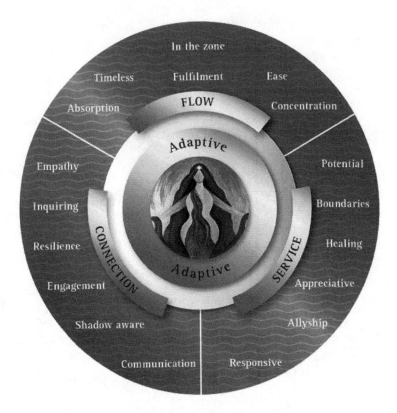

Figure 5 Luminary Interconnectedness

Connectrix

At the centre is Connectrix, reminding us of the importance of experiencing your Goddess Gnosis and of seeing the world through the lens of interconnectedness.

Adaptive

In the purple and silver circle is adaptive, the Luminary water state of being. This involves being highly responsive in your actions and responses to others, through empathy and emotional intelligence. When you are adaptive you are agile, in flow and aware of your impact on others. Your heart feels inclusive, open, wise and flexible. You can communicate easily and respond flexibly to whatever context you find yourself in, even in complex situations when there are no easy solutions available.

You are willing and able to learn new skills and behaviours in response to changing circumstances, and to stay open to whatever is presented. You learn to let go of, or to amend, anything you may have planned, if it no longer feels appropriate. You feel comfortable with experimentation, making mistakes and learning from them without blame or guilt. Many of the challenges faced today cannot be solved with what we already know from experience, or with simple solutions, because the pace of change is now much quicker. Luminaries are flexible, responsive and adaptive.

* * *

There are three sections: flow, service and connection, with six facets in each.

Flow

[Flow means] Being completely involved in an activity for its own sake. The ego falls away. Time flies. Every action, movement, and thought follows inevitably from the previous one, like playing jazz. Your whole being is involved, and you're using your skills to the utmost.
Mihaly Csikszentmihalyi (Geirland, 1996)

We all are capable of reaching a state of effortless concentration and deep absorption, with a sense of ease in which we are so completely involved in an activity that it feels timeless. A state that generates connection, fulfilment, enjoyment and high skill. This state is called 'flow' and is similar to the feeling of being deeply present or fully interconnected. In the state of flow, ordinary preoccupations fall away, time flies, every action, movement and thought follows on naturally and easily from the previous one, and your skills function at their optimal. Flow is an act of moving smoothly, naturally and easily. It may be a steady movement through writing, singing or playing a sport, or the movement of a river. Being in flow takes you from seeing everything as separate pieces into a sense of the whole.

Flow can be a spiritual experience of your Goddess Gnosis, something deeply mystical. It is also very practical and can be actively developed. For the Luminary, conscious development of flow in themselves, in others and in community can foster powerful engagement, high skill and significant accomplishment. Flow can happen when engrossed in almost any activity: reading, meditating, dancing, running, or playing your favourite sport or a musical instrument. It is estimated that one in five people say that flow happens to them as much as several times a day, whereas others say that this never happens to them.

I have identified six facets of flow: in the zone, timelessness, ease, fulfilment, absorption and concentration.

These build on the work of Csikszentmihalyi in *Good Business: Leadership, Flow and the Making of Meaning* (2003) and *Flow: The Psychology of Optimal Experience* (1990), as well as my experiences of flow. I believe everyone is capable of developing and experiencing all of these. Flow can happen spontaneously or through consciously developing it; with practice it can be more continuous.

Exercise

1. Sit and viscerally remember a time of flow or imagine one; get deeply in touch with it.
2. If you are feeling blocked here now, not flowing, identify what needs healing in you to flow more.

3. Remember a time when you experienced flow.

4. What did it feel like? What was significant about that experience for you?

5. Reflect on how walking in nature affects the feeling of flow in you.

6. How do you experience Goddess as flow in your life?

7. Find a Goddess chant you love and sing it repeatedly until you experience flow.

8. Now reflect on what happened during this exercise.

9. What did it feel like? What was/is significant for you?

10. Write in your journal.

The six facets of Luminary Flow

In the Zone

Being in the zone, or deeply present, is the sensation of being completely in the moment or in a state of intense focus. When you are in the zone, you forget the world around you and are totally focused on your current task or experience. One way of expressing flow is that you are no longer dancing: you are the dance (or running or singing or doing a work task). Being in the zone can help you to perform at very high levels, with ease. Getting caught in your emotions can tumble you out of the zone. While hard to describe, you know when you are in it.

Timelessness

Timelessness, by its very definition, refers to something unaffected and unchanged by time. It is the quality of not feeling affected by the process of time passing. Time moves, of its own accord, into a different dimension from linear time. It feels different in the sense that you have no conscious notion of how long you may have been doing something. An hour may seem like three seconds. After a timelessness experience you may say that "the time flew by", as you were so absorbed. In this state, time loses any relevance or importance.

Ease

Have you ever experienced something feeling very easy and happening with very little effort on your part? Your mind may have felt free of mental clutter or busyness, and you knew exactly what to do without worrying or fretting. This is the feeling of ease when there is no difficulty, blockage or need to strain or make conscious effort. You notice an absence of stress.

Fulfilment

This involves enjoying an activity for its own sake, knowing that the way in which you approach something, or someone, is as important as any result. When fulfilled you feel deeply happy, content and satisfied, as well as creative and productive. You can feel filled up with everything you need: no more yearning or longing for something or someone else.

Absorption

This is the place where you are so deeply involved in an activity that you become assimilated, integrated, or absorbed into it completely. The task and you feel as though they have become one. Nothing else seems to matter or is noticed as you are so fully engrossed in your experience. You may feel fascinated, interested and involved with all your energy and attention. It's a deeply beautiful experience and can feel graceful and inspiring.

Concentration

This is the ability to think carefully about something you are doing and nothing else, to be able to focus and not get distracted. Focusing on your breath may help if you struggle to concentrate. Martial arts practitioners understand somatic concentration in a deeply profound way: learning to focus not only on your mind, but also your whole body. The more relaxed the state of your mind and body, the more likely it is that you will stay focused, avoid distractions and achieve your goals in the process.

Reflection

1. Which facets are you strong in?
2. Which do you need to develop?
3. Take one strong facet and celebrate how well you do this by writing in your journal, drawing, painting, making a sculpture, creating a poem or a song.
4. Take one facet you need to develop and reflect on what you will do, change or improve.

Service

The word 'service' has multiple connotations but in a Luminary context involves the action of helping or doing work for someone else, acts of assistance, support, healing or kindness. In essence, caring deeply about others and being willing to pay attention to and to serve their needs. The words 'service' and 'leader' in conventional hierarchical leadership approaches may be considered an oxymoron, yet combined in a meaningful and sincere manner, service supports Leaderful behaviours.

Some people, especially women, can be triggered by the words 'servant' or 'service' as they relate them to being diminished or abused. I am using 'service' in the liberated meaning of genuine motivation and a deep desire to serve by supporting, understanding and empowering others. It's important for women to be clear about the differences between genuine service, which comes from a conscious, intentional and liberated place, and sacrifice or servitude. Service involves and develops resonance and the relational qualities of the heart, including empathy, compassion, deep listening and awareness of your impact on others. It involves managing your own reactivity, behaving skilfully and valuing everyone involved. This way of leading can ensure the inclusion of multiple viewpoints through liberating structures and processes in community.

In his doctoral thesis about my work, Michael Joseph (2002) records how he witnessed my genuine desire to be "of service, to care and love", which affected others by breaking through their mistrust and previous experiences so that they "felt able to take risks, stick their heads above the parapet and realise more of their potential".

Service is supported by self-esteem in your own worth, ability and contribution. It requires clarity about your personal values, ethics and beliefs and the capacity for loving self-acceptance and acceptance of others while holding the importance of the task and meeting necessary deadlines and community outcomes. Luminaries steeped in service see through to the connection, unity and harmony of what, at our deepest common purpose, unifies everyone in meaningful and productive behaviours.

Reflection

1. As a leader, who and what are you serving and why?
2. What are you in service to right now?
3. Is your leadership an expression of what you value most deeply?
4. How can you express service through Goddess in an explicit way?
5. Do those you serve grow as people?
6. How do you lead for positive effect on the least privileged in society?
7. How can you work towards the healing of others?

The six facets of Luminary Service

Potential

Seeing into the potential of others, even when they cannot

see it for themselves, is such an important ability. It requires an understanding that people have an intrinsic value beyond anything they may be able to do here now. It also involves seeing the talent and possibilities available. It is central to being a Luminary, one who births the potential of others. When part of your leadership, it involves a deep commitment to the personal, professional and spiritual growth of every individual in your community. Commitment to fostering the potential of others turns leadership into being truly Leaderful. Being able to see your own potential is important too. We will explore in Cycle VI how, when we are manifesting our fullest potential, we can foster, facilitate and encourage the fullest potential of others. Expressing fullest potential and possibility without hubris or exaggeration is important.

Boundaries

For many people, especially women, it can be difficult to know how to hold your own boundaries in relationships. For those of us brought up to accommodate constantly the needs of others, our ability to know our own needs can be complex. Saying yes too often can lead to depletion of energy and resentment. It is important to get clear about what you want, and don't want, from others. When you have healthy boundaries, you don't put up barriers, or close down; instead, you can state clearly without guilt, apology, blame or shame what matters to you. Useful questions to ask yourself in any relationship include:

- Is my yes given fully and freely, with some reservations or grudgingly?
- Am I receiving or just tolerating?
- Is the other person really listening to me when I say what I want?

When you are present and centred, it is easier to know and hold your boundaries and to listen to all the signals from your mind, heart and gut.

Healing

A subtle sense of healing can be communicated simply through the mutual understanding and commitment between two or more people that they are supporting each other's potential and wholeness. Sometimes it's the small things that help others to heal and be receptive, such as a gesture of support, appreciation or understanding. Learning to be a conscious healer can be a powerful service for transformation and integration as a Luminary. Developing your healing capabilities to optimise the potential for healing yourself and others is not everyone's choice, but I genuinely believe everyone has the capability to be a healer in different ways, energetically or otherwise. Think about the ways in which you are a healer and what the word means to you. Find your own unique way of being a healer. I regularly give and receive spiritual healing, as well as receiving body massages. Looking after your own wellbeing, health and healing is important.

Appreciative

This involves the feeling of being grateful. It involves the ability to understand the worth, quality or importance of, and being able to appreciate, something or someone. I always remember reading about the power of appreciation and since then I have actively learned how to appreciate others. I know it's something that I like to receive. It must be real, appropriate and sincere. For some, it is an easy thing to do; for others it may be hard. It involves noticing what has been given by another, then showing how much you appreciate it. Words are often the main way, but if appropriate, small gifts can say more than words. Things I have discovered really matter to people are sending handwritten notes of appreciation and going to them personally to say thank you. In all my courses, we do appreciation practices. Draw on the power of appreciation by giving simple but sincere thanks, acknowledging achievements and giving small tokens; sincere appreciation can bring deeper connection.

Allyship

To ally means to unite or form a connection or relation between. Authentic allyship is given by someone from a non-marginalised group who uses their privilege to advocate for a marginalised individual or group. They transfer, in some way, the benefits of their privilege to those who lack it. Being an ally involves significant self-awareness, humility and understanding of others. It involves actively and consistently challenging, unlearning and re-evaluating your own specific position of privilege and power. The purpose of doing this is to support someone else, hopefully alongside a commitment to ending the system of oppression in which we all find ourselves. Being an ally requires deep trust, sensitivity, humility, resilience and a commitment to continual learning. It is not about you, or an identity to hold. It's about serving, supporting and enabling others, in ways they choose to ask for. It is not about offering support and solidarity in a way that isn't helpful, isn't wanted or that actively harms. That is called 'performative allyship', a situation in which a self-appointed ally wants to receive some kind of reward for being a good person or wanting to be on the right side.

Responsive

Our capacity to respond is much greater if we are authentic and open-hearted. The more we love and accept ourselves, the more we can do the same for others, without any sense of resentment or limitation. The word 'responsibility' means the ability to respond, response-ability. You demonstrate respect to others by responding to them as fully and as quickly as you can. If you don't respond to others, they may feel ignored or may not reach out to you again. I am a huge fan of giving constructive, and if necessary, challenging feedback to others on a regular basis. It shows you are noticing, understanding, and are willing to give attention to, another person.

Reflection

1. Which facets are you strong in?
2. Which do you need to develop?
3. Take one strong facet and celebrate how well you do this by writing in your journal, drawing, painting, making a sculpture or creating a poem or a song.
4. Take one facet you need to develop and reflect on what you will do, change or improve.

Some facets will come naturally to you, while others may take practice; the more you practise, the better you will become.

Connection

The more we tune in to an unfolding interrelation with another, the more we can embrace the co-creative dance.
Giles Hutchins (2016, p. 137)

Practising presence, mindfulness and open-heartedness through meditation, self-awareness and reflection are important parts of the connecting journey. To co-create resonance and good relationships, listening deeply and knowing the right questions to ask is far more important than believing you should have all the right answers. To relate better with others, I have explored a wide range of intelligences, particularly emotional intelligence (EI).

The notion of intelligences has been around for many years. Daniel Goleman made the concept of emotional intelligence mainstream and popular within leadership development.

* * *

Leadership is relational. It's all about trust and building relationships together to work towards a common purpose. Leaders inevitably impact the emotional states of people around them positively through consistent, constructive relationships and emotions. Connected leaders inspire others and adjust emotionally to the energy and rhythms of individuals and groups. Leaders have little ability to control people. As well as co-creating safety, they need to build environments and networks of connection through which people are motivated and attuned to others' behaviours and feelings.

The six facets of Luminary Connection

Empathy

Empathy is the ability to feel what others feel, understand what others have to say and be attuned to subtle social signals about what others need or want. It helps you to understand, accept and recognise how someone else is feeling, or why they are reacting the way they are. People with empathy are more able to support others. Empathy is a key part of emotional and spiritual intelligence and fosters resonance, and an atmosphere of care and support. It is important to learn how to balance deep empathy for the situation with also being able to get things done and deadlines met. Having clear boundaries through which you can empathise, while keeping in touch with your own needs, is an important skill.

Inquiry

Inquiry, curiosity and the ability to explore options and ask good questions is more important than believing you know or have clarity in an unknowable complex environment. Inquiring and continually listening is a significant part of the Luminary teachings. It really helps if you can practise Luminary maieutic listening, as explored in Cycle II. This is designed to help you listen deeply and intently, soul to soul, to others. Deep and skilful listening, combined with skilful inquiry and wise questioning, is very powerful and can be liberating for others.

Resilience

Life is full of twists and turns, from everyday challenges to traumatic events that can affect you deeply and can have a lasting impact. People respond to change and trauma differently, and usually adapt well over time to life-changing events and stressful situations. The way someone adapts and recovers is in part thanks to their levels of resilience. Resilience is the process of adapting well in the face of adversity, trauma, tragedy, threats or significant sources of stress. Becoming more resilient helps you to get through difficult circumstances and to recover and bounce back. It can also involve profound personal growth and bring new insights to improve your life. Being resilient doesn't mean that you don't experience difficulties or distress: it can be those very difficulties that help you to develop strength and capacity to bounce back. Increasing your resilience involves behaviours, thoughts and actions that anyone can learn and develop; for some, though, it may take time and practice.

Engagement

Engagement is the extent to which people feel involved with, and passionate about, their work. How much they are committed to the collective, and will give, voluntarily, their discretionary effort and energy. Emotional connection can encourage motivation. It is important to understand what people value and what enables them to feel a sense of belonging and contribution. True engagement cannot be forced, only fostered. This is a highly significant facet for people being highly energised and genuinely wanting to speak positively about the collective. Those who draw referent power frequently have very engaged people around them. The level of your own engagement will influence the engagement of others. The more you are genuinely engaged, the more flow, service and connection are likely to happen.

Shadow Aware

I have placed this here to name the importance of having awareness of our shadow. This is covered in Cycles III and V. You will go deep into your shadow and toxic leadership in Cycle V. Unconscious bias and microaggressions lie in our shadow, so we need to work to reveal them by noticing when and how we treat others discriminatively. They can be changed or interrupted through honest self-exploration, feedback and practice. This work needs compassion and sensitivity, because shaming, blaming and outing may increase defences rather than dissolve them. Change begins with you and your motivation to change yourself. It is important to move through your unconscious bias into conscious bias so that you have connection and understanding in working with others. Bias itself is not the issue; it's when bias is used to discriminate, oppress or marginalise that it becomes a problem.

Communication

Good communication skills are essential to allow others, and you, to understand information more accurately and quickly. In contrast, poor communication leads to frequent misunderstanding and frustration. When communicating with others, you may focus on what *you* should say. However, effective communication is less about talking or telling, and more about listening. Listening well means not just understanding the words or the information being communicated, but also understanding the emotions the speaker is trying to convey. You could also work on recognising people's body language and trying to see situations from differing points of view, as well as offering helpful feedback and constructive criticism.

Reflection

1. Which facets are you strong in?
2. Which do you need to develop?
3. Take one strong facet and celebrate how well you do this by writing in your journal, drawing, painting, making a sculpture or creating a poem or a song.
4. Take one facet you need to develop and reflect on what you will do, change or improve.

   Some facets will come naturally to you, others may take practice; the more you practise, the better you will become.

Embodiment Practice

1. Spend time by, or in, water. This can include wells, the ocean, lakes or rivers. Be deeply present and notice how the water affects you. I take students to the Chalice Well and White Spring in Glastonbury where we can immerse in their waters.
2. How do you feel the flow and adaptability of water?
3. How does being in water affect you?
4. Create your own ceremony to honour the element of water.

Closing Songs

Find some sea or water music that enables you to dance easily and to flow with it.

Sea and water music I like includes:

- 'Song of Healing (Wave Sounds Nature Music)'[43]
- 'The Sea' by Krystalwerk[44]
- 'Dancing Path: Flowing' by Gabrielle Roth[45]
- 'Sentimental Music (Background Music)' by Yoga Waheguru.[46]

1. Dance to the music you choose from your heart, letting it move your body.
2. Use a veil or a scarf; move it with your hands, let it flow around you, above you.
3. Become the flow of the scarf or veil. Finish in your own time.
4. Did you lose yourself in the music, in the movement, in the moment?
5. How is your heart here now?
6. How are you feeling? Which word or sentence best captures your experience?
7. Take time to write about your experience in your journal.

Closing Reflection

Now take time to reflect on all you have learned and experienced in this Cycle. Let it integrate within you. Revisit anything you feel isn't yet complete. When you feel ready, in your own time, move into the next Cycle.

Cycle V The Brilliance of Dark Moon

Wisdom Keeper

She who is wise, deep, fierce and true, transforming and guiding. She is ancient, dark and bright, showering gifts from the deep. Seeing clearly beyond all filters of personality, shadow, wounding and reactivity.

Dimensions
Archetype: **Wisdom Keeper**
Direction: **North-West**
Moon: **Dark**
Path of Power: **Fierce**
State of Being: **Wisdom**
Way of Knowing: **Shadow**

Themes
Shadow, Luminary Archetypes Shadow Characteristics, Projection, Toxic Leadership, Dark Goddesses, Luminary Gold

Introduction

In the Luminary training, it was the shadow work together with understanding and exploring the Enneagram that really dropped me into deep truths. I am so grateful, Lynne. This work showed me where and how I allowed my helpfulness to others, my own feelings and the feelings of others to be disempowered, overlooked, ignored and even excluded. I am now able to lead from the emerging future within the web of grandmothers weaving. Feeling my soft power, walking gently and gracefully in my energy and actions to co-create and lead from the heart.

Angie, Goddess Luminary

At the north-west is dark moon and the archetype of Wisdom Keeper: She who is wise, deep, fierce and true, transforming and guiding. She is ancient, dark and bright, showering gifts from the deep. Seeing clearly beyond all filters of personality, shadow, wounding and reactivity.

This Cycle supports you to gain greater clarity about anything that gets in the way of your capacity to manifest all the archetypes, especially Illuminatrix. In this journey, you will find and express the brilliance of dark moon to create more space for your own shining, fullest potential, authenticity, power and brilliance. You will understand your shadow, toxic leadership and how you may be projecting on to others from your unconscious. You will spend time with the power and wisdom of Dark Goddesses and explore the shadow side of the Luminary archetypes.

Some of us have done considerable work on the wounded, shadow or unconscious parts of ourselves. For others, this may be a new arena of exploration. Wherever you are in your process, treat yourself with deep respect, find support if you need it and keep safe.

Wisdom Keeper helps you to traverse your depths and to find

your own innate wisdom. This Cycle is designed to encourage you to see those parts of yourself that need to be seen and let go of, or relaxed enough, that you can more fully understand and access all the dimensions of the Luminary Wheel.

In this Cycle you will:

- open up more deeply to your shadow
- find your own inner gold and wisdom
- explore your relationship to dark moon and Dark Goddesses
- reflect on your capacity for projection and reactivity
- explore the Luminary archetypes shadow model
- understand the importance of doing your shadow work
- learn how to stop projecting on to others
- understand how to survive toxic leadership.

Feel free (or not) to wear black or dark colour clothes for any part of this Cycle.

Being Present

Before beginning the work of this Cycle, take time to be present in whatever way suits you best. Centre yourself, by sitting, standing or walking, indoors or outdoors.

Notice your breathing, your posture and where your attention is. How deep can you go internally? How much is your attention drawn outwards? Go as deep and centred as you can.

Notice your thoughts; can you notice them without being drawn into them?

It is important to feel safe during the deep work you will be doing.

Please practise self-care and take space to relax or move out of the work if you need to, at any point. Wrapping yourself in blankets and lying down may help. Let Dark Goddesses hold and guide you. Remember to keep present.

Three Dark Goddess chants I particularly like are:

- 'Kali-Ma' by Kellianna[47]
- 'Hecate' by Wendy Rule[48]
- 'Song to Inanna' by Lisa Thiel.[49]

Calling In

In your own way, call in one or more of the Dark Goddesses.

Create an altar and place items that say something you want to share about your relationship with darkness and your shadow, or that help connect you to dark moon, any experiences of toxic leadership or a specific Dark Goddess.

Checking In

Check in with where you are now; perhaps write in your journal or just notice and be aware of what is happening for you inside and out, here now. Stay as present as you can and notice what is happening in your body. Being aware and conscious of your inner state is important for this Cycle. It may help to walk on the land, or have a trusted friend available, when doing some of the exercises.

Shadow

What is Shadow?

Our unconscious bias, constrictions and reactive personality qualities are called the 'shadow' because you cannot see them. They sit beyond your sight, in unknown or unseen parts of yourself. Shadow is usually associated with negative aspects. You can also hold your finest qualities in your shadow. By refusing or being unable to own either, you cause them to be projected on to others. Your shadow includes the things about yourself that you deny, the things your caretakers, culture, peers or communities didn't want, approve of or accept, in you. Anything subdued, criticised or deemed unacceptable.

The word 'shadow' is a 'mythological' name invented by Carl Jung. A useful metaphor is "our shadow bag", a term created by Robert Bly in *A Little Book on the Human Shadow* (1988). Your shadow bag fills up in the first half of life, as a depository for all those characteristics of personality that are disowned. You may spend up to 20 years putting content into your shadow bag and the rest of your life retrieving, revealing and healing the contents to restore your wholeness. Everyone makes choices not to be a certain way in the world, for good reason: usually, to maintain emotional, physical or spiritual 'safety' in a family or other context.

Consciously or unconsciously, you have put certain unwanted thoughts, feelings and behaviours into your shadow bag. Sometimes your energy may burst out, uncontrollably and unexpectedly. It feels as though this energy is in control of you or has no connection with who you really are.

To be truly whole, you need to identify all your destructive behaviours, thoughts and actions. Few people like to talk about the negative parts of themselves because it doesn't make anyone feel good. Many self-development, leadership and spiritual approaches focus on elevating, which can lead to bypassing and not bringing your internal darkness into the light. Luminary shadow work, in contrast, seeks to ground you so that you can acknowledge both your negative and positive qualities, then learn how to integrate them. Shadow work is an important part of learning to be deeply skilful, responsive rather than reactive.

How Do You Experience Your Shadow?

Do you find yourself in situations behaving in a way you don't want to behave, doing what you don't want to do, and saying things you don't want to say? Perhaps feeling as if you are out of control? This is because an energy or wounding, which you placed unconsciously into your shadow bag as a child, from a particular experience, has remained within you. It is now being activated in a current situation; the situation, in some way, mirrors the original situation from your childhood. Your outburst or reactivity, with a strong energetic charge, can feel draining and constricting; it feels as though you are in its control. It de-energises and diminishes your responsiveness, magnificence and confidence. It can prevent you from being appropriate and skilful.

Shadow energies can make anyone behave in ways that cause difficulties in relationships, leading to low self-esteem and self-criticism. They may manifest as strong emotions: anxiety, guilt, depression, shame, rage, jealousy, sadness and so on. They are irrational; you may say things you regret. You may not understand what comes out of your shadow, and you may repeat dysfunctional, unhelpful, unexpected and unwanted thoughts, feelings and behaviours. These shadow energies stop you being who you truly are.

Shadow is easier to see in others than in yourself and is problematic only if you don't explore, acknowledge and understand it. Phyllis Chesler's *Woman's Inhumanity to Woman* (2001) is a fascinating book, which explores why and how women hurt each other because of a wide range of societal and interpersonal influences.

Why Face, Understand and Release Your Shadow?

Shadow work can increase your energy and free you up, mentally, emotionally and physically. To honour and accept one's own shadow, in all its facets, can be a profound leadership and spiritual discipline. The aim is to fully access every part of your psyche rather than using your energy to repress parts of yourself that were unwanted or unsafe to express in your childhood. Through healing your shadow, you can become the person you were always meant to be. To own your shadow, genuinely and fully, is to reach equanimity and to gain balance and acceptance of both the light and dark in ourselves. Shadow work brings insight and, eventually, a resolution to any problems that arise from unrecognised tensions within yourself. You resolve those internal commentaries and anxieties that are constantly running inside you. You experience greater inner freedom to pause and make conscious choices. You put an end to any behaviours that no longer serve you or anyone else.

Shadow work has two parts: first, the process of getting to know the various aspects and dimensions of your personality, of which you are unaware; second, reclaiming and integrating these disowned parts back into your conscious behaviours, intentions and character.

Luminary Archetypes Shadow Characteristics

Bringing the shadow to awareness reduces its destructive power and releases the life energy stored in it.
Tsultrim Allione (2009, p. 21)

Everyone has a shadow side, even the Luminary archetypes, so let's begin our exploration of shadow by exploring their shadow (see Figure 6 on the next page). For each Luminary archetype, I list a shadow name and a set of shadow qualities. I offer this as a way to begin exploring shadow in a slightly more impersonal way, as this may be easier for some people.

Illuminatrix: DiminisHer

Makes small, reduces, constricts, ignores, dismisses, saps energy, shrinks, occupies the space of others, takes from, neglects, disregards, forgets, generates deficit or feels self-diminishment internally.

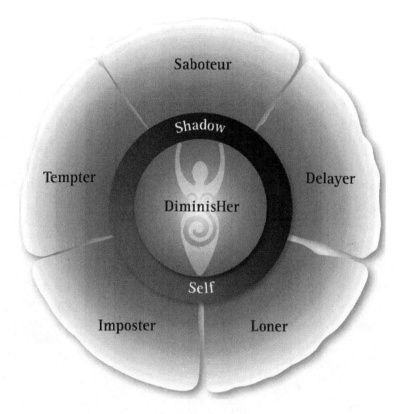

Figure 6 Luminary Shadow Archetypes

Initiatrix: Saboteur

Spoils, thwarts, fails to manifest, doesn't complete or fulfil projects or commitments, things don't happen, blocks, prevents, frustrates. If becomes Tyrant then destroys, criticises, blames, gives 'putdowns', humiliates, ridicules, shames.

Ignitrix: Delayer

Prevents, procrastinates, slows, confuses, misses deadlines, gets distracted, dishonours or fails commitments, slows things down, merges, avoids confrontation, cannot be on time, frustrates, fuzzy boundaries, scatty, doesn't complete on time but may complete.

Connectrix: Loner

Individualist, self-centred, disconnected, doesn't consult, does their own thing regardless of others, underplays, floats away, doesn't listen, is out of sync, narcissistic, cannot maintain intimacy, disappears, cold, impersonal, withdraws.

Maturtrix: Imposter

Inauthentic, fake, feels not real or will be 'found out', unstable, erratic, incongruent, uncertain, walks on eggshells, nervous, afraid, presents to others through grandiosity or smallness rather than authentic self.

Wisdom Keeper: Tempter

Indulges, makes unhealthy or unwise choices or decisions, may have addictions, self-indulgent, steps into affairs not their business, interferes, no filters, indulges others rather than challenges healthily.

Exercise

1. Sit with a mirror and look into your own eyes, look deep, see what you see.
2. How do you relate to each of the Luminary archetype shadow characteristics above?
3. Write down what of your own shadow you can see in the characteristics.
4. Which characteristics particularly resonate with you; which don't?
5. Can you see anything else that is hidden inside you?
6. Journal about your learning and insights.

* * *

7. Choose one shadow characteristic to work with.

8. Reflect on how it manifests in your life, or leadership.
9. Move physically in a way to express it.
10. How does it make you move?
11. How does it feel?
12. Think more about how you can reveal and release this characteristic.
13. How can you allow the experience of this characteristic without shame, guilt or fear?

Projection

To honor and accept one's own shadow is a profound spiritual discipline. It is whole-making and thus holy and the most important experience of a lifetime.
Robert A. Johnson (1993, p. 120)

Projection is a psychological defence mechanism that people unconsciously employ to protect themselves from difficult feelings, emotions, insecurities: any undesirable feelings.

Unless you do conscious work, as in the exercises above, your shadow will be projected. This means that you send it outside yourself and place it on to someone else. You do this when it's too painful to take ownership or responsibility for what exists in you. It is important to remember that you do this in complete innocence, so please do not blame or be harsh with yourself. We all do it; it's part of being human. What you reject or ignore inside will manifest in your external world until you see, release and heal it. This behaviour may insulate you from criticism, but it also deflects from authentic self-reflection and genuine transformation and taking responsibility for all aspects of yourself.

You can also project your own unintegrated virtues, values and goodness on to others, by placing them on a pedestal or ignoring any weaknesses or limitations they have. This can further delay your development and may do damage to another by burdening them with your darkness, or your light. A way in which you can access and see the contents of your shadow bag is by noticing how you are placing particular qualities into the world, and outside yourself. Much of what you perceive in others and in the outside world are actually parts of your projection.

It is important also to take responsibility for your own lack of skilfulness and not fall into the trap of making everything you do about someone else. The key lies in noticing when you are out of control, overreacting or feeling full of charge. Sometimes a challenge to what you are doing can be appropriate. Some new age paths make everything about someone else's shadow rather than learning how to receive skilful, appropriate and timely feedback, as an objective truth, when behaviour may fall short in some way. I am focused on helping you to understand your shadow, so you don't fall into this trap. It's important to become really clear about what belongs to you, and what belongs to someone else's shadow bag.

I have developed checklists for you to become aware of what might be happening in a relationship or situation, and how you may be beginning to project by becoming reactive, responding with charge or losing your equanimity. I hope you find them valuable. The checklists include specific things you can be, or do, to stay present and clear when you have fallen into projection.

They are part of a set of six Luminary cards to enable you to feel equipped and Leaderful, explained in Chapter 5.

Luminary Checklists to Manage Your Projection

In Your Interactions

- Be deeply present, self-aware and authentic.
- Feel love and compassion for others involved.

- Feel your autonomy and set appropriate boundaries.
- Don't let your boundaries be violated.
- Be confident in speaking your truth without charge.
- Be accurate with your perspective.
- Listen as a maieutic Luminary.
- Remain adaptable and seek feedback.
- Stay open to changing your views.
- Have constructive suggestions to offer.

Are You Projecting?

- **Are you responding with charge?** There is an emotional charge, loss of control, discharging, your voice is too loud or soft, body language is withdrawn or aggressive, you feel constriction in your body.
- **Are you colluding?** There is a sticky or murky feel to what you are doing; your boundaries are merged or confused, not really speaking your truth.
- **Are you accommodating?** You speak from fear, or feeling a need to survive, pleasing or calming the other, avoiding your truth in case it creates conflict; your boundaries feel violated.
- **Are you punishing?** You are consciously, or unconsciously, seeking or getting revenge for your wounding, feeling resentment, attacking, however unintentionally.

After Any Interaction

- Are you deeply present and clear in your truth?
- Are your boundaries unviolated?
- Is the issue closed for you or does it remain open?
- Do you still have issues running inside you?
- Would you like to suggest a clearing conversation?

Exercise

1. Can you recall any experiences in which you have projected on to others?
2. What have you learned in this Cycle that will enable you to do better or differently?
3. Reflect upon any experiences of being projected on to, and any reactivity you had.

Toxic Leadership

The Luminary Wheel is all about developing and encouraging non-toxic, ethical and skilful Leaderfulness, so it's important to understand what toxic leadership involves. The term 'toxic leadership' refers to leaders who are leading primarily out of their shadow. The pressures of leading can make you so stressed that your shadow takes over and you create toxic cultures, which disempower rather than liberate.

I believe that toxic leaders are frightened leaders who have developed ineffective behaviours to cover their irrational fears and haven't learned how to work with their shadow bag. They can complicate, drain your energy, irritate, distract, waste time, stress you out or derail your projects. Those who can recognise and challenge, circumvent or change toxic leaders will be in the best position to protect themselves, and to be effective. The issue is not simply a matter of individual survival. Toxic leaders divert people's energy from the work of the organisation or community, lower morale and interfere with cooperation and information sharing. The first book I read on this topic was *The Allure of Toxic Leaders: Why We Follow Destructive Bosses and Corrupt Politicians – and How We Can Survive Them* (Lipman-Blumen, 2006), when I was working in a very unhealthy, and painful, college environment.

Stepping into a leadership role can involve drawing significant projection from other people on to you. It's romantic, exciting and comforting to think of leadership as being all about inspiration, decisive action and rich rewards. Yet leading may involve taking risks, putting yourself on the line, disrupting the status quo, and bringing hidden conflict to the surface. Any of these things can cause people to resist and push back, for their shadow to be stimulated. If this happens, you may be adversely affected, attacked even. It has happened to me numerous times, especially when bringing about significant changes. At its best, projection is complex; at its worst, it's painful, and can be very confusing. It is important to be well prepared and to do your own shadow work. All the development you have done up to now, in previous Cycles, has prepared you for these shadow explorations.

In *Leadership on the Line: Staying Alive through the Dangers of Leading*, Heifetz and Linsky (2002) show how it's possible to lead without being marginalised or derailed. They describe four strategies that are often used to challenge leaders and involve shadow behaviours: to marginalise, divert, attack or seduce. They offer everyday tools that give equal weight to the dangerous work of leading change and the critical importance of personal survival. Through vivid stories from all walks of life, they present straightforward strategies for navigating the difficulties of leadership. Helpful suggestions are provided on how to recognise and avoid being sidelined by such behaviours. I offer my own below, but you may also like to explore their book.

* * *

So how have I experienced toxic leaders? You may want to listen to the podcast of a lecture I gave on my experience of toxic leadership at Huddersfield University.[50]

In my experience, the behaviours of toxic leaders include leading from fear, control, manipulation and protectionism.

They haven't done their shadow work and may have no awareness of their negative impact upon others. They often draw on power over, and their self-interest drives their actions, choices and agendas. Some of them know that, and still do it, while others are not aware they are doing it. I have worked for leaders who were great to work for, yet others were difficult, selfish, neglectful or interfering. Some abused their power for their own ends.

Having noticed the toxic behaviour of others, I also acknowledge my own. With my coach, I worked on a range of negative aspects of my own personality. These included acting too fast, being overly convinced that certain projects and new innovations were the right thing to do, forgetting to consult sufficiently, being overenthusiastic, being too keen to be at the leading edge, going with flavours of the month that were not adequately tested, taking too many risks and being overly experimental. I could be exasperated with those I perceived as not caring enough, or insufficiently pulling their weight. I did not respond patiently or diplomatically enough with civil servants and could not hide my irritation with people I felt did not do their best for their students. I went to coaching in a genuine attempt to keep my shadow in check and I learned to apologise to staff for any unskilful behaviours. I decided early on in my career that I would never treat another living being the way that I had been treated by many toxic leaders. I knew how horrible and upsetting being mistreated in the workplace could be.

* * *

I offer 10 ways to survive toxic leaders. I am really experienced in surviving them and I would not have succeeded in my career if I hadn't found ways to survive.

Surviving Toxic Leaders

1. Watch and learn how not to do things in the toxic way that they do.
2. Learn how to get things done despite them.
3. Challenge them in ways they can hear without losing face.
4. Create oases of safety and creativity with staff you are responsible for.
5. Appoint staff in your team with strong values and courage.
6. Offer constructive dissent.
7. Find support, such as mentoring or coaching.
8. Be clear about your boundaries and articulate them.
9. Use appropriate procedures, if necessary, and keep records.
10. As a last resort, leave the situation temporarily or permanently.

An awful leader can teach you how not to do things. It's important to create an oasis of creativity and safety with staff. That is something which I learned to do early on. Work out what you can protect your team from, and what you can't. Be honest about what is possible and work together to deal with the things you cannot keep away from them. Using self-awareness tools can help you to work out other people's world views and motivations.

Reflection

1. Reflect on how you have been affected by toxic leaders and how you have survived or thrived.
2. What would you include in your survival list?
3. Reflect on the practical suggestions in the surviving

toxic leaders list above.

4. How might you draw on them in your own situation?
5. How can you ensure you are not a toxic leader?
6. What work do you need to do on yourself?
7. How can you actively support, empower and liberate others through your leadership?

Dark Goddesses

A journey to the Dark Goddess is a sacred endeavour to visit the depths of your soul, and arise reborn.
Jane Meredith (2012, pp. 218–19)

In this Cycle, I want to explore and celebrate the power, strength and beauty of darkness. In ancient times, the dark was seen as the source of all wisdom, the darkness from which all creation is birthed. It didn't have racist or negative connotations; it was simply working with the black found in nature, not within societal constructs of race and hierarchy. White people need to be highly aware of their personal understanding of Dark Goddesses, and to explore any unconscious bias, as addressed in Cycle IV. In my experience, Dark Goddesses are not bad, negative or frightening. As I understand it, their role is to teach you to understand your depth, your unconscious, and to challenge and help you to move past your fears. They can also give the strength to face some of the more painful and unavoidable things in life.

In *Burning Woman* (2016), Lucy Pearce invites you to be in touch with, or to imagine, a softer dark than the frightening masculine dark you may have been brought up with. A darkness that is soft, benevolent, unconditionally loving, holding, caressing, round and safe. She experiences this as "the loving darkness of our mother's womb". She acknowledges that for some the womb was not a safe place and they may have mother wounds, which estrange them from a loving connection with the female: a connection, or disconnection, which needs to be healed.

Exploring Dark Goddess involves meeting your own shadow and accessing the strength, wisdom and power that comes from not fearing inner or outer darkness. It can be liberating and healing to experience the loving holding and spaciousness of the dark. Dark Goddesses invoke the energy of transformation, and sometimes destruction. They can bring major life changes, unprecedented challenges and painful but necessary inner and outer shifts. It takes skill to enter their realm and underworld. It is useful to have processes, and holding, to traverse unknown inner terrain.

* * *

In *Journey to the Dark Goddess: How to Return to Your Soul* (2012, p. 1), Jane Meredith gives us wise advice:

> Dark Goddess is a mysterious and hidden figure. Although each of us is familiar with her roles of wicked witch, the crone, the bad mother, the hag and the winter queen, we don't always remember her other face of compassion, healing and rebirth. This does us a great disservice. It leaves us disconnected from the full range of the feminine divine and estranged from much of our ability to change and grow.

Dark Goddess is ignored within patriarchal gender dualities, which refuse to see female as a force of powerful, destructive and fierce energy and change. We all have nurturing sides, and we all have fierce sides. When you work with the energy and the various lessons of these powerful entities, you can learn more about all parts of yourself, and how to be more skilful, liberated and clear in your life. Her destructive aspects teach you not to fear death, especially the death of your ego, and to accept, as natural, that everyone is constantly changing and evolving. Whatever you go through in life, you can transform. Dark Goddesses also hold you in the places of death, literal or symbolic, as a natural part of the cycle of life and nature. Understanding darkness is as important as recognising the light.

Our culture has not taught us how to listen to the Dark Goddess, yet many are reclaiming and celebrating Her in many ways.

My favourite Dark Goddesses are Cerridwen, Kali, Crone, Cailleach, and Inanna in the story of her journey to the Underworld. Of the many books exploring Her, some of my favourites are:

- *Journey to the Dark Goddess: How to Return to Your Soul* by Jane Meredith
- *Mysteries of the Dark Moon: Healing Power of the Dark Goddess* by Demetra George
- *She: Primal Meetings with the Dark Goddess* by Storm Constantine and Andrew Collins
- *Return to Inanna* by Christine Irving.

Reflection

1. Reflect on what the terms 'light' and 'dark' mean to you personally.
2. What is your relationship with the dark?
3. What do you associate with the word 'darkness'?
4. What does it mean for you when you hear of Goddess as dark?
5. Find the Dark Goddesses who you most relate to and most inspire you.
6. Choose a Dark Goddess and explore Her in depth.

7. What does She help you to learn about yourself?
8. Is there anything in your unconscious bias about black that needs to be worked on?

Luminary Gold

Much of your potential and brilliance may be hidden from you, leaving you out of touch with what you are truly capable of, unable to manifest your fullest and true potential.

In *Inner Gold: Understanding Psychological Projection* (2008), Jungian author Robert Johnson aptly calls our untapped potential 'inner gold'. From a Luminary perspective, this is your Goddess within, your divinity, you at your best. Everyone has inner gold. It isn't created, but it does have to be discovered. Until it is fully revealed, you may experience depression and loneliness, envy, anger, shame or guilt. You may feel that you are a failure or obsess about what others think of you.

'Inner gold' is another term we can use for our positive shadow. In *How to Be an Adult: A Handbook on Psychological and Spiritual Integration* (1991, p. 92), psychologist David Richo explains: "To integrate the positive shadow is to acknowledge our own untapped potential behind the awe we have of others. We begin to acknowledge and to release from within ourselves the very talents and qualities we admired in others."

Your positive qualities may conflict with your conscious identity and behaviours. You may have latent natural confidence, or a keen mind or a big, caring heart. Yet these qualities may conflict with your own view of yourself, which was conditioned by your early environment. One of my positive shadow examples is that I have never been able to truly see myself as kind, despite lots of feedback telling me I am a kind person. This is because, in my family, I perceived myself as the strong one, the fighter; I often felt that I was selfish because I was the child who left and lived a very different life from my parents and siblings. Psychologists call this 'cognitive dissonance'; the mind doesn't like this ambiguity and confusion, so it doesn't know what to do with these positive qualities or how to relate to them. When we don't know how to bring these positive qualities back into us, our mind is left with only one option: to project it on to another.

Below is an exercise to reveal your inner gold, so you can manifest all of your potential and brilliance and be fully Illuminatrix.

Exercise

Reclaiming and revealing your Luminary wisdom involves becoming conscious that you are projecting your own positive qualities and brilliance on to others, instead of seeing and owning them within yourself. You will practise noticing when and with whom it occurs and how to be present to it. You can use this same process for your 'negative' shadow too.

There are seven steps:

1. Think of someone you admire or envy. Make a list of qualities or attributes you admire or envy about them. Choose *one* to work on.
2. Reflect individually on the following:
   - What would it look like if you embodied that quality right now in your leadership?
   - How would you behave differently? What new actions might you take? How would you feel?

Reflect on how embodying this quality can affect your leadership. For example, if you are working with the quality of inspiration you admire in someone, focus on practical examples of how your leadership will transform when you reclaim this power inside yourself.

3. Brainstorm at least one thing you can do each day to strengthen that quality in yourself.

4. Reflect individually on what you have learned in the previous three steps.

5. Share with a trusted friend, or journal, what you have discovered and any insights.

6. Consider how you can lead in a way that manifests this quality as an integral part of you.

7. Reflect on and journal about your whole experience.

I want you now to spend time focusing on your wisdom.

Exercise

1. How do you express your wisdom in the world?
2. Ask a trusted friend the following questions:
   - Do you see wisdom in me?
   - If so, how does it express itself?
   - If you had to describe me to someone, what would you say?
   - In what ways have I helped you in life?

Dark Moon

The dark moon is the first phase after the full moon occurs. It lasts roughly seven days, with the illuminated part of the moon decreasing each day until you see a last quarter moon. A perfect time of releasing and letting go. Dark moon occurs when the moon ends its waxing in the dark and begins its waning in the dark. The duration of a dark moon varies between 1.5 and 3.5 days, depending on its ecliptic latitude.

Embodiment Practice

1. Walk or dance in the moonlight and feel the effect of the dark moon's rays. Feel the dark of night. See the beauty and power of the darkness all around you.

2. How does this affect you?

3. What happens to your energy?

4. What does it feel like?

5. What was significant for you?

6. Write about your experience in your journal. Perhaps compose a poem or a song about it, or create a drawing, painting or sculpture.

7. Find a trusted person to share your experiences with.

* * *

8. On another night, create a simple ceremony of surrender, letting go and releasing anything that may still be hindering or blocking your own shining brilliance and your fullest Illuminatrix. Name all that you can let go of into the darkness.

Closing Chant

Listen and dance to 'Crone Song' by Touch the Earth.[51]

Closing Reflection

Now take time to reflect on all you have learned and experienced in this Cycle. Let it integrate within you. Revisit anything you feel isn't yet complete. When you feel ready, in your own time, move into the next Cycle.

Cycle VI Maturing in Abundance and Sovereignty

Maturtrix

She who is conscious of her sovereignty and dignity, who leads, supports and behaves in the fullness of all She can be. Liberating others and co-creating the best outcome for all involved.

Dimensions
Archetype: **Maturtrix**
Direction: **West**
Element: **Earth**
Moon: **Full**
Path of Power: **Through**
State of Being: **Authentic**
Leaderful Way: **Emergence**
Way of Knowing: **Body**

Themes
Luminary Styles, Luminary Shadow Styles, Luminary Sovereignty, Embodiment, Leadership Embodiment, Emergence, Final Integrative Reflection

Introduction

There are patterns and webs and weavings – lines of becoming all around me…the world is *alive*.
Sharon Blackie (2018, p. 69)

At the west is full moon, the element of earth, and the archetype of Maturtrix: She who is conscious of her sovereignty and dignity, who leads, supports and behaves in the fullness of all She can be. Liberating others and co-creating the best outcome for all involved.

This Cycle is designed for you to experience your Sovereignty. To really own your magnificence and your capacity to manifest to your fullest potential. Being truly Leaderful and skilled in fostering the blooming of others. It is the place on the Luminary Wheel of abundance, maturity, prosperity and being grounded and embodied. The more you can be reverently embodied, the more appropriate, responsive, skilful and impactful you will be.

Goddesses of Earth can help you to integrate and ground all your learning through direct experience of the element of earth, walking the land and exploring labyrinths.

I have created a Luminary Styles model to help you explore your own leadership style and to expand your repertoire. An important part of being Leaderful involves a conscious way of behaving appropriately to the context you are in, the people involved and the situation faced together with others. The more you lead from power through others, the more you will foster the shining, birthing and fullest flowering of everyone around you.

In this Cycle you will:

- know your fullest potential and Sovereignty
- feel integrated in your ways of doing, being and leading
- open up to leading from being present in your body
- explore your experience of the earth and full moon
- reflect on your capacity for developing and manifesting Luminary Leadership styles
- continue practising reflection and presence, becoming truly centred and grounded
- integrate your learning.

Feel free (or not) to wear gold, brown or earthy colour clothes for any part of reading and exploring this Cycle.

Being Present

Before beginning, take time to get present in whatever way suits you best.

Centre yourself, by sitting, standing or walking, indoors or outdoors.

Notice your breathing, your posture and where your attention is. How deep can you go internally? How much is your attention drawn outwards? Go as deep and centred as you can.

Notice your thoughts; can you notice them without being drawn into them?

You may like to begin with a body prayer. You may already have a body or movement practice such as t'ai chi, walking meditation, yoga or sacred dance. You may wish to drum and dance to this powerful chant: 'Deep into the Earth' by Jana Runnalls.[52]

Calling In

In your own way, call in the element of earth or one or more earth Goddesses: whatever feels 'right' for you. You may want to create an altar on which you place items of significance to you as you work through the themes and explorations. Place items that say something you want to share about your relationship with your body and your sovereignty, or that help connect you to the element of earth or a specific Earth Goddess. Be aware throughout this Cycle which Goddesses are guiding and influencing you.

Checking In

Check in with where you are now, before you work through any part of this Cycle; perhaps write in your journal or just notice and be aware of what is happening for you inside and out, here now. Stay as grounded as you can and notice what is happening in your body. It may help to walk on the land whenever you can.

Luminary Styles

Looking through the lens of your leadership styles is used widely in mainstream leadership development. A range of approaches are available. I found a Hay profile of my leadership styles invaluable in understanding myself and my impact on others. The broader your range of styles, the more expansive, responsive, effective and appropriate you can be. The aim is to be able to draw on several different leadership styles, whichever fits a situation best.

I have developed a model of Luminary styles to explore your behaviours and ways of relating to others. Everyone develops their own way of behaving and responding, as a leader, based on their experiences, preferences, capabilities and personality. The overall way and flavour of how you lead, and the way in which you are seen to lead, is your style. You need to be mindful of which style fits, or not, within the context, community, movement or organisation you are in. I have witnessed leaders with an overly strong or rigid style enter a new community and their style clash with the values and culture already in place. Understanding your own preferred style and being open to developing and accessing a range of styles is important.

You clarified your own authentic way of leading in Cycle II and being adaptive in Cycle IV. Both are important in understanding how your behaviours affect others.

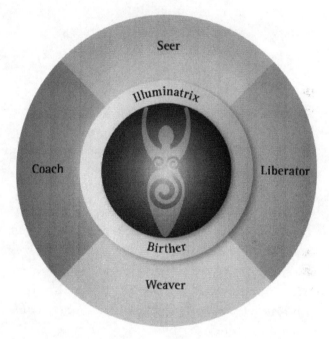

Figure 7 Luminary Styles

In my model of the Luminary styles (Figure 7), Goddess is at the centre, reminding you to be present and centred in your own unique Goddess Gnosis. In the inner circle are Illuminatrix and Birther; they hold and guide you.

The four Luminary styles in the quadrants are Seer, Liberator, Weaver and Coach.

By understanding each of these four Luminary styles of leadership, you can understand yourself better, discover areas in which to improve, and expand your repertoire of styles. You can also identify other ways of leading that may better serve your situation. They may also help you to understand how to work with others who follow a different style from your own.

Illuminatrix

Illuminatrix keeps your clarity unobscured and shining through insight, wisdom and an uncluttered clarity of perspective. She enables creativity and the achievement of purpose, tasks and roles.

Birther

Birther keeps you conscious of the importance of birthing the potential of others, as well as the fullest potential of yourself. She helps you to birth, in any situation, the most appropriate style or mix of styles.

Seer Style

Seer is the most visionary style. This style helps you to keep seeing and holding the bigger vision and purpose of any endeavour. This is the style of the founder and initiator, the person who understands where the collective needs to go. This style has a future focus. The seer may be full of new ideas, too many sometimes. They may be the more visible and in-front kind of leader.

Liberator Style

This style encourages innovation and creativity. It has an action focus and wants to get things done as quickly as possible. It fosters self-organising processes and autonomy and may have a feel of urgency. At best, this style can create high trust and feel empowering. It wants rules, process and procedures only when necessary, not for their own sake. They may be the leader who is in or alongside the team, with their sleeves rolled up.

Weaver Style

This style is highly relational. The focus is on developing constructive relationships, understanding people's emotions and knowing what motivates others. It can feel inclusive and caring. At best, it fosters a healthy balance of people and task, but may be too friendly and informal for some people. It sees the networks and patterns between people and in collectives. This style welcomes and celebrates diversity. This leader will be highly visible and like being a part of the community. They may encourage social gatherings and activities.

Coach Style

This style is one of supporting, developing and enabling the individual and collective potential. This style genuinely wants to foster everyone's ability, authenticity and fullest potential. It will have a feel of co-creating, and that we are all in this together. It may be more hands-off than the other styles, and less visible. It works primarily through others, rather than a pacesetting upfront approach. This is the leader who you can turn to and share with, who will always listen.

Reflection

1. Which styles do you use most frequently today?
2. Which styles are you strongest in?
3. Which styles do you not use, or need developing?
4. What can you do to move yourself towards your integrated expression of the styles as appropriate?
5. Journal about your insights and any actions you will take to make changes in your style of leadership.

Luminary Shadow Styles

Each style has both positive and potentially negative behaviours. Read the descriptions in Figure 8 below which lists the shadow, or negative aspects and behaviours, of each of the Luminary styles.

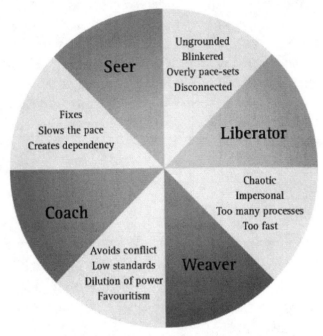

Figure 8 Luminary Shadow Styles

You may want to add behaviours that you know you manifest but are not included here.

You will go deeper into what is shadow and shadow work in Cycle VI.

Reflection

1. Can you see yourself in any of the shadow styles listed above?
2. How do they manifest?
3. What impact do these behaviours have on yourself and others?
4. Are you ready to explore how you can heal your shadow

styles?

5. If so, what might you do to develop or change your behaviours to enable this to happen?

6. What wounds might you need to heal?

Embodiment Practice

I invite you to find and explore labyrinths. Search online and find an outdoor labyrinth near your home, or one to which you can travel. If you cannot find one on the land, draw a labyrinth or find a hand labyrinth you can experiment with. You may want to read about the history and practice of labyrinths. I have walked labyrinths all over the world. I love this fascinating and profound spiritual practice of meditatively walking in sacred space on the land. I have a chamomile labyrinth in my own garden and walk it regularly. If you are new to labyrinths, you may find some links in the Online Resources section useful:

- *How to Walk a Labyrinth*[53]
- *New to the Labyrinth?54*
- *The 3 R's of Labyrinth Walking*[55]
- *How to Draw a Classical Labyrinth*[56]

Once you have experienced a labyrinth, reflect on:

- What happened for you? What did it feel like? What was significant for you?
- Write about your experience in your journal. Compose a poem or song about it, or create a drawing, painting or sculpture.

Luminary Sovereignty

I encourage you now to explore and embody your Luminary Sovereignty, to feel your fullest potential, authenticity and power, while being deeply grounded in the land. Everyone is connected with all of nature. You are nature, you are Goddess, and She is you. Being able to experience yourself as Sovereign, someone who lives and leads from the fullness and depth of Mother Earth, is important to being an embodied Luminary. Feel within you the space of growth, harvest, nurturing and abundance. Feel your interconnection, love, expansiveness and embodied wisdom. Luminary Sovereignty opens you to being able to express *all* the Luminary states of being: authenticity, autonomy, adaptiveness and self-awareness.

Sovereignty is not dominion. When fully in your Sovereignty, you don't take power or want power: you *are* power. There is no arrogance, apology or diminishing anyone else. You hold power, in all its healthy forms, because you want everyone else to manifest their own power and autonomy too. You know, also, the joy of serving others through generosity and love. With clear boundaries, and a dignified self-authority, you can respond skilfully, consciously and expansively in the world. You feel your deep resilience and inner strength. You can challenge and cut through all that is false and unnecessary, with compassion and composure. You fulfil, with ease, your rights and your responsibilities. You are Maturtrix, conscious of your Sovereignty and your Leaderful power. You liberate others and co-create the best outcome for all.

Having journeyed through the Luminary Wheel and all the dimensions, you are no longer overwhelmed, hiding or reactive. You are aware of, and have seen and integrated, your shadow. It feels natural to work for the interests of the greater good of the whole, of everyone, not just in your own self-interest. Sovereignty enables you to be loyal to yourself, as well as to the people and issues that matter deeply to you. You can foster success in your life, clearly vision, know your purpose and successfully manifest. You now express *all* that you are capable of, manifesting your fullest potential, fostering and facilitating the fullest potential of others.

As Luminary Sovereign, you sit in your clear and uncluttered light, being Illuminatrix, as well as Maturtrix, illuminating others, encouraging them to shine brightly.

You offer service into the world as a Leaderful Luminary through establishing and modelling post-patriarchal ways of being, drawing on all the dimensions of the Luminary Wheel.

* * *

For some, the words 'Queen', 'King', 'Queer' or 'Fluid' of their realm resonate strongly, instead of 'Sovereign'. If none of these work for you, use a different word. Feel deeply into which word works best for you. I want to be inclusive of all genders, so feel deeply into your own unique Sovereignty, within a gender identity that totally fits the expression of who you truly are. Working within the Divine female paradigm, I use 'Queen', although I identify as androgynous. Goddess honours all binary and queer identities.

The Queen (as archetype) for me is the reflection of how I see myself and my own sense of personal power. She reconnects me with my inherent goodness and strength, and my embodied and integrated wise woman. I am still in the process of accessing, healing and acknowledging my inner Queen.

Reflection

1. Explore your sense of your Sovereignty, being Queen, King, Queer or Fluid. (Use whichever word most expresses your unique Sovereignty and gender expression.)
2. How do you relate, or not, to your Sovereignty?
3. Describe how it feels and manifests in your body.
4. How do you experience your unique Sovereignty?
5. Name three qualities you manifest as a Sovereign

Luminary, ones that feel genuinely authentic and enable you to feel and express your magnificence.

6.   You may want to share these three qualities with someone else to name them publicly and to ground them in yourself.

Exercise

1.   Really feel deep into your Sovereignty.
2.   Wear something that makes you feel regal, and in your full power (a hat, crown or headdress, a dress, shirt, cloak or robe, whatever feels perfect for you).
3.   Stand as Sovereign, in your Sovereignty.
4.   Stand tall, noble, upright, authentic and regal (5 minutes).
5.   Speak words that feel right for you.
6.   Walk in your Sovereignty (at least 5 minutes).
7.   Feel your energy and power.
8.   Emanate your Sovereignty for as long as feels good and empowering to you.
9.   You may enjoy listening and walking to the chant, 'I Am the Goddess', by Lisa Thiel.[57]
10. Feel into your Sovereignty, your fullest expression of Goddess, your divinity, your magnificence expressing itself through human form.
11. Journal about how you are affected by doing some or all of the above.

Embodiment

Embodiment practices are a fundamental part of many wisdom school traditions. Goddess spirituality is a deeply embodied spiritual path. In the west and earth direction of the Luminary Wheel, you turn attention to your body. Previous Cycles have explored mind, gut and heart. This Cycle explores how you know and live through your body. It matters how you can experience your body as sacred and explore your relationship with your body. The way in which you sit and stand influences and enhances your leadership.

What is Embodiment?

Embodiment means being 'in-body', fully aware of and alive *from inside out* of your own body and physicality. Being embodied means experiencing the world through your physical body, and being deeply aware of, and connected to, nature and the earth.

Becoming embodied involves bodywork and movement practices and exploration of internal, subjective bodily experiences.

Embodiment Practice

A simple experiential way of experiencing embodiment is to:

1. Notice your hand; look at it as an inanimate object, a thing, not part of you.
2. Observe its qualities objectively. Touch it as you would an inanimate object.
3. How does this feel for you?
4. Now relate to your hand as something that is a part of you and belongs to you.
5. Jiggle your fingers, turn your hand over, look at both sides.
6. Now move both your hands at the same time. Enjoy your hands.
7. Be playful with your hands.
8. Recall the ways in which you use your hands, how your hand has been useful, the people you have touched with your hands, the many experiences you and your hands have shared.
9. How do your hands feel now, as an integral part of you?

10. Notice how this is, and how different from your first reflection it is.

    This is experiencing your own embodiment through relating to your hand as an integral part of yourself. Full embodiment is experiencing all your body as fully integral and alive.

11. Which parts of your body do you feel connected to?

12. Are there any parts you feel disconnected from?

The word 'embody' is used to describe character traits you see in a person; for example, "They embody truth" or "They are the embodiment of goodness". In the acting world, when an actor gives a compelling and recognisable representation of a character, we say they have "truly embodied" that person.

There is a strong and ancient tradition of a different kind of embodiment in the Goddess spirituality world for which embodiment involves a distinct spiritual practice and service. In this form of embodiment, priestesses open themselves to being fully Goddess in their physical bodies. They move beyond their personality defences of separation, allowing Goddess to appear in and through their bodies and become a physical expression of "I am Goddess".

If you are interested in learning more about this, I recommend *Priestess of Avalon, Priestess of the Goddess: A Renewed Spiritual Path for the 21st Century* (Jones, 2006).

Leadership Embodiment

People look to see what behaviours their leaders embody, as much as, if not more than, what they say. It helps enormously if leaders are congruent in both their actions and their words.

Out of the vast literature and teachings about embodiment, I prefer the work of Wendy Palmer. She combines the martial art of aikido with mindfulness practice. She has adapted her work to offer techniques that help leaders recognise how their minds and bodies habitually react to pressure. She supports leaders to learn how to access skilful responses in the situations they face. She acknowledges how leaders wish to remain calm and present, but in stressful situations their bodies often constrict, and they become agitated or reactive. She offers three premises:

- The body takes a shape before the mind consciously identifies a thought or feeling
- Our physical being is the most direct point of intervention
- How you sit and stand will change the way you think and speak.

While you cannot transform yourself into someone who no longer has any stress responses, Palmer's work can help you to recognise your reactive tendencies at their inception. She focuses on how, through deep awareness of your body, you can consciously move to a centred or present state, a state that enables self-regulation and the capacity to access your three brains and their aligned higher functioning, as explored in Cycle II.

I recommend *Leadership Embodiment: How the Way We Sit and Stand Can Change the Way We Think and Speak* (Palmer and Crawford, 2013). It is full of powerful exercises and insights.

If you want a quicker read, I suggest her short summary, *Leadership Embodiment: Enhancing the Wisdom of Leaders* (2017),[58] or her video, *Introducing Leadership Embodiment*.[59]

Palmer proposes a clear connection between an individual's level of wellbeing and their ability to lead well in stressful and complex environments. She believes that how well you are physically has a direct impact on what you can achieve. She explores how everyone is habituated to respond to stressors, yet you can teach yourself to recover your innate capacity for wisdom, compassion and confidence, even in stressful situations. This becomes possible with a move from contraction to expansion as your head shifts from control to perception, your heart from approval to compassion, your gut from safety to confidence. This aligns with the Sacred model in Cycle II.

Palmer has discovered that effective leaders manifest three embodied leadership competencies:

1. **Inclusiveness**, when they can expand their presence and embrace small and large audiences by creating a 'we are all in this together' feeling. I have always been naturally good at this, so I know exactly what she means. Do you? I like how Palmer relates inclusiveness to physical presence. I believe such inclusiveness is also interconnected to emotional intelligence and to openness of heart.

2. **Centred Listening**: leaders listen with their whole being, hearing all that is being said without taking the message personally. Yes! This is why Luminary maieutic listening and illumination circles are introduced in Cycles I and II, as bedrocks of Luminary development and practice.

3. **Speaking Up**: being able to speak your truth, even when it is not a popular view, with clarity and precision, without becoming aggressive or collapsing. This is so important and was explored in Cycle III, through the lens of power.

What Palmer adds to the leadership and the Luminary Wheel is learning how to manifest these three things somatically, through the way you lead in your body.

Embodiment Practices

The best way to understand your own body and be more in touch with your personal embodiment is to experiment with physical practices. I offer below an amalgam of exercises adapted from Palmer to help you improve your somatic expression as a leader.

Practice 1

1. Stand, breathe, be in your body, stay grounded.
2. What is happening in your body as you do this?
3. How do you know when you are grounded?
4. Now: uplift your posture.
5. Then: extend your personal space to fill the room.
6. How does this feel?
7. Now: relax your shoulders.
8. How do you feel?

As you do this practice, you change the way you are organising your energy. This enables you to access more parts of your brain. This simple exercise allows your brain to access its creativity, innovation and inspiration and helps you to focus. The more you repeat it, the more you can access your three brains.

9. Journal about the impact of this practice.

Practice 2

1. Think of people who are good at leading. What do you notice about their leadership presence, their non-verbal behaviour, posture, body language and, most important of all, the way they occupy their environment?
2. Write down your thoughts in your journal.
3. What do you know and feel about your own leadership presence?

Practice 3

1. Enter a room, look at the corners, assess the size of

the space and then extend your personal presence and energy to fill the room. Expand out and into the corners. Fill the whole space.

2. How does this feel?
3. Is it easy or hard to do?
4. What happens in your body when you do this?
5. Did you notice anything getting in the way of your expansiveness?

The more expansive your presence, the more anyone entering that room will be welcomed into your personal space. You will be giving them a non-verbal message of inclusion and connection.

Emergence

Emergence...is another way of speaking about the connective tissue of all that exists – the way, the Tao, the force, change, God/dess, life.
adrienne maree brown (2017, p. 3)

Emergence builds on several Luminary Wheel dimensions, particularly being adaptive, experiencing flow and alignment of our three brains. The pathway of emergence involves constantly rethinking, aligning and adjusting to what is happening in current time, taking into account new factors as they arise or are discerned. The seasons of life, and of the natural world, are cyclical. Emergence continuously unfolds through rhythms and cycles. The Luminary Wheel teaching moves through the four seasons, and includes creativity, growth, release and renewal: all aspects of emergence. Emergence requires presence, something you have practised many times. Being present enables an open mind, an open heart and an open will, alongside a relaxation of your usual personality and its preoccupations. You can go beyond your usual ways of seeing the world, with all your projections and limitations. You may even enter unknowing, as discussed in Cycle II. This allows a myriad of unseen potentials and possibilities to arise and emerge.

From the perspective of emergence, any group is viewed as having a creative spark of its own, with the role of every member being to listen to where the group dynamics want or need to go. Everyone then aligns their actions and outcomes with collective evolutionary purpose.

An important part of fostering emergence involves the capacity to see the patterns and energetics of any relationship or collective. Feeling any disharmonies and knowing when something is not quite right. Recognising and knowing when everything is flowing, and what is allowing all possibilities to arise. Books that have helped me to understand this include:

- *Emergent Strategy: Shaping Change, Changing Worlds* (brown, 2017)
- *Future-Fit* (Hutchins, 2016)
- *Regenerative Leadership: The DNA of Life-Affirming 21st Century Organizations* (Hutchins and Storm, 2019).

Reflection

1. Explore the concept of emergence and exactly what it means for you.
2. Reflect on your relationship with control, letting go and letting come.
3. How does Goddess affect your life; can you surrender to a larger sense of purpose?
4. Explore your understanding, desire and capability for working with emergence.
5. Ask yourself what gets in the way of you being fully in emergence.

6. Reflect on what personal capabilities you need to lead from emergence.
7. How have you experienced interconnectivity in nature and/or with other people?

Earth Chants

Two of my favourite earth chants are:

- 'Deep into the Earth'[60]
- 'Mother I Feel You'.[61]

1. Dance to these, being fully in your body, letting them move you with their rhythm and flow.
2. Feel your dance emerging in the flow of now.
3. Be the beat of the song; feel deep into its rhythm and beat.
4. Can you lose yourself in the music, in the movement, in the moment?
5. Finish in your own time. Then sit, breathe and relax into how you are here now.
6. When you have finished, notice how you are feeling; take time to write in your journal.

Full Moon

Full moon is when the moon has reached its zenith and forms a bright and full, perfect, silvery sphere, a time of fertility, abundance, strength, love and power. It is also the moon representing Goddess in her Mother aspect.

You may wish to dance in the moonlight and to feel the effect of the moon's rays on your body.

You may be inspired to write a poem or song or to dance.

Closing Chant

Listen and dance to 'Sisters of the Moon' by Lindie Lila.[62]

Or listen and dance to one or more of these drum music videos:

- *Full Moon Drumming Circle*[63]
- *"Arising" vocals and frame drum by Miranda Rondeau*[64]
- *Medicine Dream (Drum Reprise) by Gabrielle Roth & The Mirrors.*[65]

Closing Reflection

Now take time to reflect on all you have learned and experienced in this Cycle. Let it integrate within you. Revisit anything you feel isn't yet complete.

Final Integrative Reflection

What really matters to you? The fact that you're alive means you've been given a reprieve to think deeply about that question. How will you use what matters in service to yourself, your community, and the world?
Oprah Winfrey (Oprah Daily, 2020)

As this is the final Cycle, I encourage you to reflect on your whole journey and to integrate all that you have been learning, understanding and experiencing in the previous Cycles, as well as in this one. Such integration will enable you to let your own brilliance shine, unafraid to express your own magnificence.

1. Clarify the four most important insights or learnings about *yourself* you have gained.
2. Describe what they are, and how they will affect you, your relationships and your behaviours.
3. Clarify the four most important insights or learnings about your *leadership* you have gained.
4. Describe what they are and how they will change or

improve your leadership into the future.

5. How do you feel about being a Goddess Luminary in the world?
6. What does that mean to you in practice?
7. What is your understanding of being Leaderful?
8. What does it mean in your context, and how will you practise this?
9. What was your favourite part of the book? Why?
10. What did you find most challenging or difficult? Why?
11. What do you most appreciate about yourself? Make a list and pin it on the wall.
12. Write yourself a love letter telling yourself at least four things you most love about yourself.

When we love we can let our hearts speak.
bell hooks (2001, p. ix)

Chapter 5

Illuminating and Manifesting

Feeling Equipped and Leaderful
Maieutic Luminary Dedication
Impact and Contribution of Luminaries in the World

Personally, the Goddess Luminary training has been life changing.
It has given me so many new skills and insights. Since completing
the course, I have had a significant promotion. I firmly believe that
the Goddess Luminary training gave me the skills to put myself
forward for this new role and the self-belief that I was able to take
on such a challenge. During the two years of the training, I took
the learning, practical tools and my own insights into my NHS
team. I have utilised many elements of the course to develop my
team, including the Enneagram, clearing conversations and the
perception of power. I have even introduced the senior management
team to the concept of spiral dynamics. It really helped in
improving our team working and helped me better develop my staff
by focusing on their individual needs and talents. I feel much more
confident and skilled as a leader.

Being with others was really enjoyable, and sometimes I was
deeply challenged. I also loved seeing the other course members
develop and take forward their own insights. I loved the eclectic
mix of input from Lynne, the exercises, the ceremonies and the
energy and support of the group. I am certain I will carry my
learning from the Goddess Luminary training with me for the rest
of my life.
Lizzie, Goddess Luminary

Feeling Equipped and Leaderful

You cannot get through a single day without having an impact on the world around you. What you do makes a difference, and you have to decide what kind of difference you want to make.
Jane Goodall (Jane Goodall Institute, 2017)

I give a gift, one of many throughout the course, on successful completion to support maieutic Luminaries, beyond the course, in their professional, community and daily lives. Everyone receives a pack of six Luminary Leaderful interventions cards. Each card has one of the Luminary archetypes on it with a very practical checklist.

The Illuminatrix card supports Being in Luminary Presence and Clarity; the Wisdom Keeper card helps you to check: Are You Projecting? The other four cards each contain a practical checklist of actions, interventions and suggestions. Initiatrix supports self-reflection and really knowing your authenticity; Ignitrix guides you to stimulate and generate change. Connectrix focuses on co-creating supportive relations with others. The Maturtrix card has a checklist of suggestions to foster collective processes, and to co-create a culture of respect, safety and accountability. The Maturtrix card also prepares students who join Spiral 2. The cards can be carried around in your bag or pocket to pull out and consult when needed.

Maieutic Luminary Dedication

On completion of Spiral 1, students dedicate, as a maieutic Luminary, She or he or they who births the highest and fullest potential of themselves as a conscious and committed Luminary.

The word origin of 'maieutic' is the Greek word *maieutikos*, relating to midwifery, from *maia*, meaning midwife. We explored and practised maieutic listening and method, as I have developed it, in Cycle I. At the completion of the course, we remember the call of the 'Goddess Charge to Her Luminary', as explored in Chapter 3. As Goddess Gnosis is at the heart of the Luminary Leadership Wheel, we organise a sacred ceremony and dedicate to Goddess in whatever shape, form, name or lineage feels right for each individual. It's a very special occasion of completion and celebration.

Impact and Contribution of Luminaries in the World

I want to share what Goddess and maieutic Luminaries are doing in the world and the impact they are having, as this is a very practical journey. As a pragmatist and implementer, that's seriously important to me. As I said in my invitation at the beginning, my vision is to birth a movement of Goddess Luminaries with the motivation, power, skill and capability to make our world a better place, supporting and encouraging Luminaries to be the change they wish to see in the world.

In Spiral 1, students design and deliver a specific project out of their dreaming, visioning, passion and desire to birth something significant to them into the world. The projects have been really varied and have included creating Luminary sprays to retail, setting up new or very different businesses, expanding current work into new markets and expanding their services.

One student designed a pagan burial ground and a powerful business plan to gain funding. Several students have created new training courses or successful campaigns. Others introduced new team-building projects into their workplaces and new ways of working and felt confident to push the boundaries of the organisations and communities that they are already a part of. Several are now coaching.

A couple of students set up exciting community projects that their hearts have been yearning to do for a very long time. There were several creative projects involving sculpture and painting.

Two students expanded their work: one into establishing a new company and the other setting up a retreat on a boat. Several got promoted or moved into more senior roles. One became a non-executive on a charitable trust board, her first board appointment. Several are incorporating Luminary approaches into their own consultancy, healing and counselling practices.

The most important thing in all these projects was enhanced skill development, improved relationship building and confidence building, as well as every student realising that they have the capacity to be a skilful, compassionate and powerful leader with significant impact and contribution within their context.

I am delighted with the wide range of contexts from which the students come: chief executives of charities, university and college lecturers, a senior nurse, artists, activists, healers, writers, middle managers from private companies, priestesses, retreat owners, consultants and an interfaith minister. One person travelled from the United Arab Emirates seven times, and never missed a weekend or was late on any occasion. In the first two years, 29 people from all over the UK, the Republic of Ireland, Holland and the United Arab Emirates have attended the face-to-face programme. Forty more people from 12 different countries participated in four online sessions.

Goddess Luminaries are making a significant impact all over the world. The community I dreamed of is being co-created.

I want to end my book with words from the students; at the end of the day, it's all about them and their flourishing. I want students to have the last word in answering the question "How do I have an impact in the world and how have the Luminary teachings helped me?" Some answers are threaded through the book; you will have read them already. Here are a few more:

Thank you for another powerful and beautiful weekend. It moved

me deeply and I am still processing a lot of wonderful insights around it and loving my new connection to the word 'power'.
Dharam, maieutic Luminary

The most important gain for me personally is the ability to take the learnings from the course and apply them immediately to my working environment. The Goddess Luminary Wheel can be applied to leadership roles across all environments. I would highly recommend the training for anyone who is interested in effecting change in their own leadership style and wishes the ability to influence change in their immediate surroundings, be it personal or professional.
Alison, Goddess Luminary

Every weekend is full of practical learning combined with theoretical background, really profound work. I feel so safe and seen for who I am in this course. This training has had a huge impact on my life, so much understanding and inspiration. I wholeheartedly recommend this course to everyone who wants to lead and manifest their dreams and vision.
Katrin, maieutic Luminary

The Luminary training is an inspiring and empowering course, and I would recommend it to everyone. I began the course when I was entering the world of leadership and it helped me to find my place within it and helped me to develop my own authentic leadership style.
Iona, maieutic Luminary

I really hope you have enjoyed the book, have learned much and keep returning to taste its wisdom and flavours, again and again.

Thank you for journeying through *Goddess Luminary Leadership Wheel* with me.

May this ending also be another beginning.

May you love, be present and shine brightly as Illuminatrix
May you manifest your dreams and be deeply authentic as Initiatrix
May you feel powerful and passionate to make the world a better place as Ignitrix
May you flow and offer service from your heart, deeply interconnected as Connectrix
May you journey through your depths to find the brilliance of your wisdom as Wisdom Keeper
May you be fully sovereign and abundant in all you manifest as Maturtrix

Blessed Be

About the Author

Dr Lynne Sedgmore CBE is a former chief executive, an executive coach, organisational consultant, priestess and published poet. She offers a unique synthesis of Leadership and Goddess spirituality for our modern times. She bridged mainstream organisations and spiritual communities for over 30 years and the organisations she led won numerous awards.

She was appointed CBE for services to education and was named as one of the UK's '100 Women of Spirit' and as one of the most influential people in a Debrett's 500 list.

She is the author of three poetry books, *Enlivenment: Poems*; *Healing Through the Goddess: Poems, Prayers, Chants and Songs*; and *Crone Times: Poems*. Lynne is active in the Glastonbury Goddess community as a practising priestess, teacher and healer. She coaches individuals and senior teams in charities and organisations that inspire her. Her leadership impact, and poetry, has featured in many books, articles and magazines.

Her course is offered through the Glastonbury Goddess Temple training courses. Details can be found at https://goddesstempleteachings.co.uk/goddessluminary

From the Author

Thank you for purchasing *Goddess Luminary Leadership Wheel*. My sincere hope is that you derived as much from reading this book as I have in creating it. If you have a few moments, please feel free to add your review of the book to your favourite online site for feedback.

If you would like to connect with me further, please visit my website at https://www.lynnesedgmore.co.uk

Sincerely,

Lynne Sedgmore

Appendix

Spiral 2

Overview

The second Spiral goes deep into group processes and working within collectives. It explores and honours different perspectives within group dynamics. It is more outward-looking and includes collective change processes and broader systems thinking. Students experiment with liberating processes, self-organising systems, Teal practices, people's assemblies and empowering circles. Projects involve co-creating and manifesting change within students' own communities, cultures or movements.

Collective Goddess Luminary Leadership Wheel: Cycle I

This examines the Goddess Luminary Collective Wheel as a collective whole system and applying the Wheel in groups, communities, movements and organisations. The following themes are explored:

- Understanding group processes, reactivity, conflict and differences
- Clarifying collective projects
- Remembering your confidence, authenticity and power
- Goddess Luminary Presence
- Journeying through the Luminary change process
- Expanding awareness and holding of group fields
- Leading skilfully beyond conventional organisational forms.

Powering Collective Luminary Fire, Flow and Culture: Cycle II

This Cycle focuses on:

- Igniting collective power through shared and Leaderful interventions
- Change agency
- Reinventing organisations
- Burning through collective hubris and unconscious bias
- Illuminating deep or hidden structures and cultures of power
- Stepping deeper into collective Luminary Leaderful flow
- Dissolving and healing collective shadow
- Immunity to change.

Maturity and Abundance as Goddess Luminaries in the World: Cycle III

This Cycle focuses on:

- Co-creating healthy cultures
- Holding the energetic field
- Sustaining post-conventional forms of organisation and community
- Leading collectively from emergence
- Luminary Change model
- Maintaining sustainability and abundance in organisations.

Integration and Dedication: Cycle IV

This final Cycle focuses on:

- Gathering, integrating and harvesting everything learned, created and manifested
- Finalisation of the gathering of fruits to share and embody

as Goddess Luminary in the world
- Creating a collective Leaderful collage
- Dedication as Goddess Luminary.

Spiral 2 is offered through the Glastonbury Goddess Temple training courses. Details can be found at https://goddesstempleteachings.co.uk/goddessluminary/spiral-two/

Online Resources

Chapter 1 Return of Goddess

1   A *Call to Stand Live@TEDx Findhorn – Eleanor Brown* (2018) YouTube video, added by Eleanor Brown [Online]. Available at https://youtu.be/HPDOGmkPJkk (Accessed 16 May 2021).

2   Sedgmore, Lynne (2013) 'Fostering Innovative Organisational Cultures and High Performance through Explicit Spiritual Leadership', unpublished thesis, Winchester, University of Winchester [Online]. Available at https://winchester.elsevierpure.com/en/studentTheses/fostering-innovative-organisational-cultures-and-high-performance (Accessed 16 May 2021).

3   Joseph, Michael (2002) 'Leaders and Spirituality: A Case Study', unpublished thesis, Guildford, University of Surrey [Online]. Available at http://epubs.surrey.ac.uk/653/1/fulltext.pdf (Accessed 16 May 2021).

4   *Charge of the Goddess: Prayer to the Mother of All Living by Doreen Valiente* (2020) YouTube video, added by Spells8 [Online]. Available at https://youtu.be/X-17EIC-Dfk (Accessed 16 May 2021).

5   Christ, Carol P. (1978) 'Why Women Need the Goddess' [Keynote address to an audience of over 500 at the Great Goddess Re-emerging conference at the University of Santa Cruz] https://womrel.sitehost.iu.edu/Rel433%20Readings/Christ_WhyWomenNeedGoddess.pdf (Accessed 21 August 2021).

Chapter 2 A New Way

6   UNFPA (2020) *Impact of the COVID-19 Pandemic on Family Planning and Ending Gender-based Violence, Female Genital Mutilation and Child Marriage* [Online]. Available at https://www.unfpa.org/sites/default/files/resource-pdf/COVID-19_impact_brief_for_UNFPA_24_April_2020_1.pdf (Accessed 16

May 2021).

7   ActionAid (2020) *Impact of Covid-19 on Young Women: A Rapid Assessment of 14 Urban Areas in India, Kenya, Ghana and South Africa* [Online]. Available at https://actionaid.org/sites/default/files/publications/YUW%20final%20report.pdf (Accessed 16 May 2021).

8   Rosa (2021) *Rosa's Covid-19 Response: Preliminary Report* [Online]. Available at https://fairsharewl.org/project/feminist-leaders-for-feminist-goals/ (Accessed 21 August 2021).

9   Sedgmore, Lynne (2019) *The Luminary Leaderful Way: Goddess Luminary Wheel Teachings* [Online]. Available at https://wheresthefinleadership.s3.eu-west-2.amazonaws.com/201910_Luminary_Leaderful_Way.pdf (Accessed 16 May 2021).

10 Freeman, Jo (1984) *The Tyranny of Structurelessness* [Online]. Available at https://www.jofreeman.com/joreen/tyranny.htm (Accessed 16 May 2021).

11 Batliwala, Srilatha (2010) *Feminist Leadership for Social Transformation: Clearing the Conceptual Cloud* [Online]. Available at https://www.uc.edu/content/dam/uc/ucwc/docs/CREA.pdf (Accessed 16 May 2021).

12 ActionAid (n.d.) *ActionAid's Ten Principles of Feminist Leadership* [Online]. Available at https://actionaid.org/feminist-leadership (Accessed 16 May 2021).

13 Oxfam (n.d.) *Feminist Principles* [Online]. Available at https://oxfamilibrary.openrepository.com/bitstream/handle/10546/621064/ogb-feminist-principles-091020-en.pdf?sequence=1 (Accessed 16 May 2021).

14 Oxfam (2017) *Applying Feminist Principles to Program Monitoring, Evaluation, Accountability and Learning* [Online]. Available at https://oxfamilibrary.openrepository.com/bitstream/handle/10546/620318/dp-feminist-principles-meal-260717-en.pdf;jsessionid=E1E3F972742F4505438553BD56562D5C?sequence=4 (Accessed 16 May 2021).

15 Fairshare (2020) *Feminist Leaders for Feminist Goals: A Toolkit* [Online]. Available at https://fairsharewl.org/wp-content/uploads/2020/10/20-10-21-FS-Toolkit.pdf (Accessed 16 May 2021).

16 *Sojourner Truth's "Ain't I a Woman": Nkechi at TEDxFiDiWomen* (2013) YouTube video, added by TEDx Talks [Online]. Available at https://www.youtube.com/watch?v=eUdxsQ0Qsrc (Accessed 16 May 2021).

17 Razak, Arisika (2016) 'Sacred Women of Africa and the African Diaspora: A Womanist Vision of Black Women's Bodies and the African Sacred Feminine', *International Journal of Transpersonal Studies*, vol. 35, no. 1, pp. 129–47 [Online]. Available at http://dx.doi.org/10.24972/ijts.2016.35.1.129 (Accessed 16 May 2021).

Chapter 3 Wisdom of the Goddess Luminary Leadership Wheel

18 Sedgmore, *The Luminary Leaderful Way*.

Chapter 4 Journeying the Wheel

Cycle I Initiating Your Luminary Journey: Illuminatrix

19 *Be Still and Listen, music by Shawna Carol* (2014) YouTube video, added by HealerWomyn [Online]. Available at https://www.youtube.com/watch?v=FKlQr8UVYh0 (Accessed 16 May 2021).

20 Brown, Brené (n.d.) *Dare to Lead Hub* [Online]. Available at https://daretolead.brenebrown.com (Accessed 16 May 2021).

21 *I Am the Goddess – Lisa Thiel* (2011) YouTube video, added by Moon Lotus [Online]. Available at https://youtu.be/u8Mz0UteSmA (Accessed 16 May 2021).

22 *You Gotta Believe – Goddesses vs Moses – by Nina Paley* (2018) YouTube video, added by Monica Jay [Online]. Available at https://youtu.be/LGiWITGArLI (Accessed 16 May 2021).

23 *The Heart of the Goddess* (2018) YouTube video, added by Hallie Iglehart Austen [Online]. Available at https://youtu.be/1QdyRs3kFg8 (Accessed 16 May 2021).

24 *Be Still and Listen, music by Shawna Carol*, YouTube video.

Cycle II The Dance of Dreaming, Knowing and Awareness: Initiatrix

25 *I Have a Dream speech by Martin Luther King Jr.* (2017) YouTube video, added by RARE FACT [Online]. Available at https://youtu.be/vP4iY1TtS3s (Accessed 16 May 2021).

26 Van Eupen, Marion 'Brigantia' (2019) *Sacred Model * Luminary Leadership* [Online]. Available at https://www.marionbrigantia.com/sacredmodel-luminaryleadership (Accessed 16 May 2021).

27 Wikipedia (n.d.) *Negative capability* [Online]. Available at https://en.wikipedia.org/wiki/Negative_capability (Accessed 16 May 2021).

28 Rivera Sun (2018) *Rivera Sun's Murmuration Exercise for Leaderful Organizing* [Online]. Available at https://www.riverasun.com/murmuration-exercise/ (Accessed 16 May 2021).

29 *I Breathe the Air* (2015) YouTube video, added by Jana Runnalls [Online]. Available at https://youtu.be/AbF4az1YKC8 (Accessed 16 May 2021).

Cycle III Igniting Power, Passion and Intuition: Ignitrix

30 *Spirits of Fire Chant* (2008) YouTube video, added by Aelwyn Daeira [Online]. Available at https://youtu.be/T6ELVt48GR4 (Accessed 16 May 2021).

31 *Dancing Fire* (2015) YouTube video, added by Jana Runnalls [Online]. Available at https://youtu.be/yp40_J5bVU0 (Accessed 16 May 2021).

32 *Fire Transform Me* (2015) YouTube video, added by Kellianna Music [Online]. Available at https://youtu.be/OTIrJpjP4Wg (Accessed 16 May 2021).

33 Freeman, *The Tyranny of Structurelessness*.

34 Sedgmore, 'Fostering Innovative Organisational Cultures and High Performance through Explicit Spiritual Leadership'.

35 Joseph, 'Leaders and Spirituality: A Case Study'.

36 *Dancing Fire*, YouTube video.

37 Wineman, Steven (2003) *Power-Under: Trauma and Nonviolent Social Change* [Online]. Available at http://www. traumaandnonviolence.com (Accessed 16 May 2021).

38 Batliwala, *Feminist Leadership for Social Transformation: Clearing the Conceptual Cloud*.

39 *A Call to Stand Live@TEDx Findhorn – Eleanor Brown*, YouTube video.

40 *Helen Reddy – I Am Woman (Lyrics)* (2010) YouTube video, added by Miluzie [Online]. Available at https://youtu.be/ xwMOC5i2eRk (Accessed 16 May 2021).

41 *Full Height of Our Power* (2015) YouTube video, added by Kellianna Music [Online]. Available at https://youtu.be/ SOC2U-5xRUA (Accessed 16 May 2021).

Cycle IV The Weave and Flow of Interconnection: Connectrix

42 *Opening to Love* (2015) YouTube video, added by Sound of Ashana [Online]. Available at https://youtu.be/aglDuLBgXFA (Accessed 16 May 2021).

Sea and water music:

43 *Song of Healing (Wave Sounds Nature Music)* (2014) YouTube video, added by Rainforest Music Lullabies Ensemble [Online]. Available at https://youtu.be/fvH3RNIeu14 (Accessed 16 May 2021).

44 *The Sea* (2014) YouTube video, added by Krystalwerk [Online]. Available at https://youtu.be/wwd6zLR5_x4 (Accessed 16 May 2021).

45 *Dancing Path: Flowing* (2015) YouTube video, added by Gabrielle Roth and the Mirrors [Online]. Available at https://youtu.be/ WwQ9OCvJ5bI (Accessed 16 May 2021).

46 *Sentimental Music (Background Music)* (2017) YouTube video, added by Yoga Waheguru [Online]. Available at https://youtu.

be/5cl5nm9hSis (Accessed 16 May 2021).

Cycle V The Brilliance of Dark Moon: Wisdom Keeper

47 *Kali-Ma* (2015) YouTube video, added by Kellianna [Online]. Available at https://youtu.be/NBUbUkh7HlU (Accessed 16 May 2021).

48 *Hecate* (2015) YouTube video, added by Wendy Rule [Online]. Available at https://youtu.be/jmf98zzwf9g (Accessed 16 May 2021).

49 *Song to Inanna* (2015) YouTube video, added by Lisa Thiel [Online]. Available at https://www.youtube.com/watch?v=hk6gPfD6j48 Accessed 13 July 2021).

50 Sedgmore, Lynne (n.d.) 'The Dark or Ethical Prince: There is Always a Choice', *Ragged University* [Podcast]. Available at https://www.raggeduniversity.co.uk/2018/02/19/podcast-and-transcript-the-dark-or-ethical-prince-there-is-always-a-choice-by-lynne-sedgmore/ (Accessed 16 May 2021).

51 *Crone Song* (2015) YouTube video, added by Touch the Earth [Online]. Available at https://youtu.be/Doph_7gKkRk (Accessed 16 May 2021).

Cycle VI Maturing in Abundance and Sovereignty: Maturtrix

52 *Deep into the Earth* (2015) YouTube video, added by Jana Runnalls [Online]. Available at https://youtu.be/QDTtDB4T5gs (Accessed 16 May 2021).

Labyrinth links:

53 *How to Walk a Labyrinth* (2015) YouTube video, added by Diane Annie Mathias 'The Wonder Path' [Online]. Available at https://youtu.be/NsESX_R6nC4 (Accessed 16 May 2021).

54 Veriditas (n.d.) *New to the Labyrinth?* [Online]. Available at https://www.veriditas.org/New-to-the-Labyrinth (Accessed 16 May 2021).

55 *The 3 R's of Labyrinth Walking* (2011) YouTube video, added by Labyrinths4u [Online]. Available at https://youtu.be/

Ud7CDXHR870 (Accessed 16 May 2021).

56   *How to Draw a Classical Labyrinth* (2014) YouTube video, added by Discover Labyrinths [Online]. Available at https://youtu.be/CyEwgGuWzCI (Accessed 16 May 2021).

57   *I Am the Goddess – Lisa Thiel*, YouTube video.

58   Palmer, Wendy (2017) *Leadership Embodiment: Enhancing the Wisdom of Leaders* [Online]. Available at http://incompanyofothers.com/WordPress/wp-content/uploads/2017/05/Leadership-embodiment_Wendy-Palmer.pdf (Accessed 16 May 2021).

59   *Introducing Leadership Embodiment* (2012) YouTube video, added by leadershipembodiment [Online]. Available at https://youtu.be/jbCDOmrds0Y (Accessed 16 May 2021).

60   *Deep into the Earth*, YouTube video.

61   *Mother I Feel You* (2015) YouTube video, added by AleviDreamtime [Online]. Available at https://youtu.be/MIqVg8CM1Gg (Accessed 16 May 2021).

62   *Lindie Lila – Sisters of the Moon* (2020) YouTube video, added by Daniela [Online]. Available at https://www.youtube.com/watch?v=HMeEkyHATIM (Accessed 16 May 2021).

Drum music:

63   *Full Moon Drumming Circle* (2015) YouTube video, added by lo ol [Online]. Available at https://youtu.be/2Ufm2RMMSuc (Accessed 16 May 2021).

64   *"Arising" vocals and frame drum – Miranda Rondeau* (2008) YouTube video, added by inspiritrixx [Online]. Available at https://youtu.be/5EDqIHv_SMc (Accessed 16 May 2021).

65   *Gabrielle Roth & The Mirrors – Medicine Dream (Drum Reprise)* (2009) YouTube video, added by zvjezd01 [Online]. Available at https://youtu.be/3jpAA1e12vU (Accessed 16 May 2021).

Bibliography

Ahmed, Sara (2017) *Living a Feminist Life*, Durham, NC, Duke University Press.

Allione, Tsultrim (2009) *Feeding Your Demons: Ancient Wisdom for Resolving Inner Conflict*, Hay House, London.

Almaas A. H. (2004) *The Inner Journey Home: The Soul's Realization of the Unity of Reality*, Boston, Shambhala.

Austen, Hallie Iglehart (2018) *The Heart of the Goddess: Art, Myth and Meditations of the World's Sacred Feminine*, revised edn, Rhinebeck, NY, Monkfish Book Publishing Company.

Autry, James (1991) *Love and Profit: The Art of Caring Leadership*, London, Chapmans.

Barrett, Ruth (ed.) (2016) *Female Erasure: What You Need to Know about Gender Politics' War on Women, the Female Sex and Human Rights*, Lebec, CA, Tidal Time Publishing.

Barton, Tracy R. (2006) 'A Feminist Construction of Leadership in American Higher Education', unpublished doctoral dissertation, Toledo, University of Toledo.

Beard, Mary (2017) *Women & Power: A Manifesto*, London, Profile Books.

Beck, Koa (2021) *White Feminism*, London, Simon & Schuster.

Belenky, Mary Field; Clinchy, Blythe McVicker; Goldberger, Nancy Rule; and Tarule, Jill Mattuck (1986) *Women's Ways of Knowing: The Development of Self, Voice, and Mind*, New York, Basic Books.

Blackie, Sharon (2016) *If Women Rose Rooted: A Life-Changing Journey to Authenticity and Belonging*, Tewkesbury, September Publishing.

Blackie, Sharon (2018) *The Enchanted Life: Unlocking the Magic of the Everyday*, Tewkesbury, September Publishing.

Bly, Robert (1988) *A Little Book on the Human Shadow*, New York, HarperCollins.

Bown, Geraldine (2017a) *On the Path to Authentic Leadership: The OPAL Way to Leadership Success*, CreateSpace.

Bown, Geraldine (2017b) *Reclaim Your Power*, CreateSpace.

brown, adrienne maree (2017) *Emergent Strategy: Shaping Change, Changing Worlds*, Edinburgh, AK Press.

Brown, Brené (2018) *Dare to Lead: Brave Work, Tough Conversations, Whole Hearts*, London, Penguin Random House.

Bryson, Valerie (2021) *The Futures of Feminism*, Manchester, Manchester University Press.

Chesler, Phyllis (2001) *Woman's Inhumanity to Woman*, New York, Thunder's Mouth Press.

Christ, Carol P. (1992) 'Why Women Need the Goddess' in Christ, Carol P. and Plaskow, Judith (eds) *Womanspirit Rising: A Feminist Reader in Religion*, New York, HarperCollins.

Christ, Carol P. (1997) *Rebirth of the Goddess: Finding Meaning in Feminist Spirituality*, New York, Routledge.

Christ, Carol P. (2003) *She Who Changes: Re-imagining the Divine in the World*, New York, Palgrave Macmillan.

Christ, Carol P. and Plaskow, Judith (eds) (1992) *Womanspirit Rising: A Feminist Reader in Religion*, New York, HarperCollins.

Constantine, Storm and Collins, Andrew (2018) *She: Primal Meetings with the Dark Goddess*, Stafford, Megalithica Books.

Crenshaw, Kimberlé (1989) 'Demarginalizing the Intersection of Race and Sex: A Black Feminist Critique of Antidiscrimination Doctrine, Feminist Theory and Antiracist Politics', *University of Chicago Legal Forum*, vol. 1989, no. 1, art. 8.

Csikszentmihalyi, Mihaly (1990) *Flow: The Psychology of Optimal Experience*, New York, Harper and Row.

Csikszentmihalyi, Mihaly (2003) *Good Business: Leadership, Flow and the Making of Meaning*, New York, Basic Books.

Daly, Mary (1973) *Beyond God the Father: Toward a Philosophy of Women's Liberation*, Boston, Beacon Press.

Delap, Lucy (2020) *Feminisms: A Global History*, Chicago, University of Chicago Press.

D'Souza, Steven and Renner, Diana (2014) *Not Knowing: The Art of Turning Uncertainty into Opportunity*, London, Lid Publishing.

Feminism and Religion (2012) *Who is She? The Existence of an Ontological Goddess By Molly* [Online]. Available at https://feminismandreligion.com/2012/09/29/who-is-she-the-existence-of-an-ontological-goddess-by-molly-meade/ (Accessed 16 May 2021).

Feminist (n.d.) *A Speech by Johnnetta Cole: The Power of Diversity* [Online]. Available at https://www.feminist.com/resources/artspeech/genwom/powerofdivers.html (Accessed 27 July 2021).

Fry, Louis W. and Altman, Yochanan (2013) *Spiritual Leadership in Action: The CEL Story*, Charlotte, NC, IAP Press.

Gaard, Greta (ed.) (1993) *Ecofeminism: Women, Animals, Nature*, Philadelphia, Temple University Press.

Garza, Alicia (2020) *The Purpose of Power*, London, Doubleday.

Geirland, John (1996). 'Go with the Flow', *Wired Magazine*, no. 409 [Online]. Available at https://www.wired.com/1996/09/czik/ (Accessed 28 July 2021).

George, Demetra (1992) *Mysteries of the Dark Moon: Healing Power of the Dark Goddess*, San Francisco, HarperOne.

Gimbutas, Marija (1974) *The Goddesses and Gods of Old Europe, 7000 to 3500 BC: Myths, Legends and Cult Images*, London, Thames and Hudson.

Gimbutas, Marija (1989) *The Language of the Goddess: Unearthing the Hidden Symbols of Western Civilization*, San Francisco, Harper and Row.

Goffee, Rob and Jones, Gareth (2006) *Why Should Anyone Be Led by You? What It Takes to Be an Authentic Leader*, Boston, Harvard Business School Press.

Goleman, Daniel (1998) *Working with Emotional Intelligence*, London, Bloomsbury.

Greenleaf, Robert K. (2002) *Servant Leadership: A Journey into the Nature of Legitimate Power and Greatness*, London, Paulist Press.

Harper, Susan (2017) 'The Future of Goddess', in Greenfield, Trevor (ed.) *Seven Ages of Goddess*, Winchester, Moon Books.

Heifetz, Ronald and Linsky, Marty (2002) *Leadership on the Line: Staying Alive through the Dangers of Leading*, Boston, Harvard Business School Press.

hooks, bell (1981) *Ain't I a Woman? Black Women and Feminism*, London, Pluto Press.

hooks, bell (2000) *Feminism is for Everybody: Passionate Politics*, London, Pluto Press.

hooks, bell (2001) *All About Love: New Visions*, New York, HarperCollins.

hooks, bell (2009) *Reel to Real: Race, Class and Sex at the Movies*, New York, Routledge.

Hutchins, Giles (2016) *Future-Fit*, CreateSpace.

Hutchins, Giles and Storm, Laura (2019) *Regenerative Leadership: The DNA of Life-Affirming 21st Century Organizations*, Royal Tunbridge Wells, Wordzworth Publishing.

Hyland, Clive (2017) *The Neuro Edge: People Insights for Leaders and Practitioners*, St Albans, Panoma Press.

Integral Life (n.d.) *Lead with Purpose* [Online]. Available at https://integrallife.com/lead-with-purpose-training (Accessed 27 July 2021).

International Women's Development Agency (IWDA) (2019) *Srilatha Batliwala: What Makes Me Hopeful* [Online]. Available at https://iwda.org.au/srilatha-batliwala-what-makes-me-hopeful
(Accessed 16 May 2021).

Irving, Christine (2018) *Return to Inanna*, CreateSpace.

Jane Goodall Institute (2017) *#EatMeatLess for People, Other Animals, and the Environment* [Online]. Available at https://news.janegoodall.org/2017/11/22/eatmeatless-people-animals-environment/ (Accessed 28 July 2021).

Johnson, Robert A. (1993) *Owning Your Own Shadow: Understanding the Dark Side of the Psyche*, San Francisco, Harper.

Johnson, Robert A. (2008) *Inner Gold: Understanding Psychological Projection*, Kihei, HI, Koa Books.

Jones, Kathy (2006) *Priestess of Avalon, Priestess of the Goddess: A Renewed Spiritual Path for the 21st Century*, Glastonbury, Ariadne Publications.

Joseph, Michael (2002) 'Leaders and Spirituality: A Case Study', unpublished thesis, pp. 182–5, Guildford, University of Surrey.

Kendall, Mikki (2021) *Hood Feminism: Notes from the Women White Feminists Forgot*, London, Bloomsbury.

Kidd, Sue Monk (2002) *The Dance of the Dissident Daughter: A Woman's Journey from Christian Tradition to the Sacred Feminine*, New York, HarperCollins.

Kite, Tracy (2018) *Love to Lead*, St Albans, Panoma Press.

Le Guin, Ursula K. (1969) *The Left Hand of Darkness*, New York, Ace Books, Grosset & Dunlap Company.

Lipman-Blumen, Jean (2006) *The Allure of Toxic Leaders: Why We Follow Destructive Bosses and Corrupt Politicians – and How We Can Survive Them*, New York, Oxford University Press.

Lorde, Audre (1982) *Zami: A New Spelling of My Name*, Watertown, MA, Persephone Press.

Lorde, Audre (1995) *The Black Unicorn: Poems*, New York, Norton.

Meredith, Jane (2012) *Journey to the Dark Goddess: How to Return to Your Soul*, Winchester, Moon Books.

Oprah Daily (2020) *Oprah's Class of 2020 Commencement Speech: "What Will Your Essential Service Be?"* [Online]. Available at https://www.oprahdaily.com/life/a32492831/oprah-commencement-speech-2020-full-transcript/ (Accessed 26 July 2021).

Palmer, Wendy and Crawford, Janet (2013) *Leadership Embodiment: How the Way We Sit and Stand Can Change the*

Way We Think and Speak, CreateSpace.

Parker, Patricia (2006) *Race, Gender, and Leadership: Re-Envisioning Organizational Leadership from the Perspectives of African American Women Executives*, New York, Psychology Press.

Pearce, Lucy (2016) *Burning Woman*, Cork, Womancraft Publishing.

Raelin, Joseph (2003) *Creating Leaderful Organizations: How to Bring Out Leadership in Everyone*, San Francisco, Berrett-Koehler.

Raelin, Joseph (2010) *The Leaderful Field Book: Strategies and Activities for Developing Leadership in Everyone*, Boston, Nicholas Brealey Publishing.

Richo, David (1991) *How to Be an Adult: A Handbook on Psychological and Spiritual Integration*, Mahwah, NJ, Paulist Press.

Rippon, Gina (2019) *The Gendered Brain: The New Neuroscience That Shatters the Myth of the Female Brain*, London, Bodley Head.

Riso, Don Richard and Hudson, Russ (1999) *The Wisdom of the Enneagram: The Complete Guide to Psychological and Spiritual Growth for the Nine Personality Types*, New York: Bantam Books.

Saini, Angela (2018) *Inferior: The True Power of Women and the Science That Shows It*, London, Fourth Estate.

Sedgmore, Lynne (2001) 'Emotional Intelligence: The Hidden Advantage', *Academic Leadership*, vol. 8, no. II, pp. 16–20, Mesa, AZ, Chair Academy.

Sedgmore, Lynne (2013) 'Fostering Innovative Organisational Cultures and High Performance through Explicit Spiritual Leadership', unpublished thesis, Winchester, University of Winchester.

Sedgmore, Lynne (2019) *The Luminary Leaderful Way: Goddess Luminary Wheel Teachings*, Glastonbury, TheaSpeaks Press.

Sedgmore, Lynne; Bishop, Rosie; Pearcy, Lorna; Turnbull, Sharon; and Williams, Ian (2021) '"Feminist Leadership" – a post patriarchal paradigm', *Thought Leadership* [Series of papers], Fownhope, Caplor Horizons [Online]. Available at https://tinyurl.com/79dt9psp (Accessed 21 August 2021).

Serano, Julia (2005) *On the Outside Looking In...: A Trans Woman's Perspective on Feminism and the Exclusion of Trans Women from Lesbian and Women-only Spaces*, Oakland, Hot Tranny Action.

Sjöö, Monica (1999) *Return of the Dark/Light Mother or New Age Armageddon: Towards a Feminist Vision of the Future*, Austin, TX, Plain View Press.

Sjöö, Monica and Mor, Barbara (1987) *The Great Cosmic Mother: Rediscovering the Religion of the Earth*, New York, HarperCollins.

Stanton, Elizabeth (1895) *The Woman's Bible: Part I.*

Stanton, Elizabeth (1898) *The Woman's Bible: Part II.*

Starhawk (1979) *The Spiral Dance: A Rebirth of the Ancient Religion of the Great Goddess*, New York, HarperCollins.

Starhawk (1991) *Truth or Dare: Encounters with Power, Authority and Mystery*, San Francisco, Harper.

Starhawk (2006) *The Earth Path: Grounding Your Spirit in the Rhythms of Nature*, New York, HarperOne.

Starhawk (2011) *The Empowerment Manual: A Guide for Collaborative Groups*, Gabriola Island, BC, New Society Publishers.

Steinem, Gloria (1994) *Moving Beyond Words: Age, Rage, Sex, Power, Money, Muscles: Breaking Boundaries of Gender*, London, Bloomsbury.

Torbert, William R. (1991) *The Power of Balance: Transforming Self, Society and Scientific Inquiry*, London, Sage.

Torbert, William and Associates (2004) *Action Inquiry: The Secret of Timely and Transformational Leadership*, San Francisco, Berrett-Koehler.

Walker, Alice (1983) *In Search of Our Mothers' Gardens: Womanist*

Prose, San Diego, Harcourt.

Ward, Tim (2006) *Savage Breast: A Man's Search for the Goddess*, Alresford, O Books.

Wheatley, Margaret (2017) *Who Do We Choose to Be? Facing Reality, Claiming Leadership, Restoring Sanity*, San Francisco, Berrett-Koehler.

Wiggins, Joy and Anderson, Kami (2019) *From Sabotage to Support: A New Vision for Feminist Solidarity in the Workplace*, San Francisco, Berrett-Koehler.

Wigglesworth, Cindy (2012) *SQ21: The Twenty-One Skills of Spiritual Intelligence*, New York, Select Books.

Williams, Liz (2020) *Miracles of Our Own Making: A History of Paganism*, London, Reaktion Books.

Winslow, Barbara (2013) *Shirley Chisholm: Catalyst for Change* (Lives of American Women), Boulder, CO, Westview Press.

Zohar, Danah and Marshall, Ian (2000) *SQ: Spiritual Intelligence: The Ultimate Intelligence*, London, Bloomsbury.

TRANSFORMATION

The Power of Being Co-Active in Work and Life
Karen Kimsey-House & Ann G Betz
Integration examines how we came to be polarized in our
dealing with self and other, and what we can do to move from
an either/or state to a more effective and fulfilling way
of being.
Paperback: 978-1-78279-865-1 e-book: 978-1-78279-866-8

How to Lead a Badass Business From the Heart
The Permission You've Been Waiting for to Birth Your Vision
and Spread Your Glitter in the World
Makenzie Marzluff
An entrepreneurship blueprint for the spiritual community to
materialize their dreams through ancient wisdom
Paperback: 978-1-78904-636-6 ebook: 978-1-78904-637-3

Savage Breast
One Man's Search for the Goddess
Tim Ward
We think of God as male, but the most common representation
of the divine through our history has been female, as the
Goddess. When did this major change happen, why, and how
has this affected relationships men and women ever since?
Paperback 978-1-90504-758-1 e-book: 978-1-78099-060-6

Lead Yourself First!
Indispensable Lessons in Business and in Life
Michelle Ray
Are you ready to become the leader of your own life? Apply
simple, powerful strategies to take charge of yourself, your
career, your destiny.
Paperback: 978-1-78279-703-6 ebook: 978-1-78279-702-9

Ripening Time
Inside Stories for Aging with Grace
Sherry Ruth Anderson
An indispensable guidebook for growing into the deep places
of wisdom as we age.
Paperback: 978-1-78099-963-0 ebook: 978-1-78099-962-3

Resetting Our Future: Rebalance
How Women Lead, Parent, Partner and Thrive
Wendy Teleki, Lisa Neuberger Fernandez &
Monica Brand Engel
Insights from a decade-long conversation among working
moms about making a difference at work, loving our families,
contributing to our communities and nourishing ourselves.
Paperback: 978-1-80341-042-5; e-book 978-1-80341-043-2

Readers of ebooks can buy or view any of these bestsellers by
clicking on the live link in the title. Most titles are published
in paperback and as an ebook. Paperbacks are available in
traditional bookshops. Both print and ebook formats are
available online.
Find more titles and sign up to our readers' newsletter
at http://www.johnhuntpublishing.com/transformation
Follow us on Facebook at https://www.facebook.com/
Changemakersbooks